sk New Yorkers where to get the best cheesecake...chances are they will send you to Junior's! Cheesecakes are what we are famous for—especially our plain New York Original that's straightforward, homemade, and simply the creamiest one you have ever tasted. But we are about much more than heavenly cheesecakes. Junior's is known for all of the fabulous food that New Yorkers love to eat, especially desserts: from towering ice cream sodas to Black & White Cookies, from four-layer skyscraper cakes to fresh berry shortcakes, from delicious sugar-free cakes to just-baked pies bursting with fruit and served your own way: plain, warm, with whipped cream, or à la mode.

Like my Grandpa Harry always said, folks should have the very best, whenever, wherever, they want it. So even if you can't drop by Junior's for dessert, you can make some of our favorites from these recipes to serve to your family and friends. And enjoy: "All you want... as you want it."

Alan Rosen
Third-Generation Owner
Junior's

Desserts

All of the recipes, text and photographs in this collection were taken from the book *Junior's Dessert Cookbook*, by Alan Rosen and Beth Allen, published by The Taunton Press, 2011. The book was edited by Pamela Hoenig, designed and art directed by Carol Singer, and photographed by Mark Ferri. The food stylist was Leslie Orlandini and the prop stylist was Francine Matalon-Degni.

The following manufacturers/names appearing in *Junior's Desserts* are trademarks: Cherry Coke®, Coca-Cola®, Famous® Chocolate Wafers, Fox's u-bet®, Ghirardelli®, Hershey®'s, Hershey®'s Cocoa, Mr. Goodbar®, Marshmallow Fluff®, Nabisco®, Nestlé®'s Toll House® chocolate morsels, Nilla® Wafers, Oreo®, PHILADELPHIA® cream cheese, QVCSM, Reese's®, SodaStreamTM, Splenda®, Torani®

Famous, Nabisco, Nilla, Oreo, and PHILADELPHIA are registered trademarks of Kraft Foods.

Issue Editor: Sarah Opdahl
Issue Art Director: Teresa Fernandes
Issue Copy Editor: Li Agen
Photographer: Mark Ferri

To contact us:
Fine Cooking
The Taunton Press
63 South Main Street
PO Box 5506
Newtown, CT 06470-5506
Tel: 203-426-8171
email: fc@taunton.com

Visit: www.finecooking.com

To subscribe or place an order:
Visit www.finecooking.com/fcorder
or call: 800-888-8286
9am-9pm ET Mon-Fri; 9am-5pm ET Sat

To contact *Fine Cooking* customer service:
Email us at support@customerservice.taunton.com

The Taunton guarantee:
If at any time you're not completely satisfied with our products you can receive a full and immediate refund. No questions asked.

Junior's Desserts: (ISSN: 1931-8227) is published by The Taunton Press, Inc., Newtown, CT 06470-5506. Telephone 203-426-8171. Canadian GST paid registration #123210981.

Printed in the USA.

Contents

The Story of Junior's

Our story begins on Cherry Street, on the Lower East Side of Manhattan. In 1895 my great-grandfather Barnett Rosen and his wife, Sarah, moved into a tenement building there from the Ukraine and got a job working twelve hours a day in the Wilson & Company slaughterhouse on First Avenue and Thirty-Eighth Street. Six children soon came along, two daughters and four sons. Grandpa Harry (Hershel), who would become the founder of Junior's, was born in 1904.

My great-grandmother, who was ten years younger than my great-grandfather, was an energetic, resourceful, and very wise woman who was always doing good deeds for others, especially her children. She taught them to seize every opportunity and to make the very best of what they had. With her encouragement, Harry and his oldest brother, Mike, worked every day after school at Marchioni's Ice Cream Parlor on Grand Street. They were allowed to spend 50 cents of their earnings each week however they wanted to; the rest their mother wisely and safely squirreled away, and in just two years Sarah saved up $1,500. With those savings, she bought the boys a partnership in a luncheonette on Duane Street and Broadway when Grandpa was only 16 and Mike 18. Later, when the owner decided to retire, they bought him out. Soon their luncheonette became known for having some of the best sandwiches and sodas in Manhattan, and they began to expand, until they owned five luncheonettes. In need of a name for the business, my Grandpa Harry thought of a manufacturer of stainless-steel luncheonette equipment called Enduro—and the Enduro Sandwich Shops were born.

Grandpa Makes the Move to Brooklyn

In the late 1920s, Brooklyn was bustling. By day, thousands of long-shoremen worked on its waterfront. Brooklyn also had a vibrant night-life, with people drawn to the beautiful Beaux Arts Albee Theater, opulent Fox Theater, and the Paramount Theater, which seated more than 4,000 and towered over the corner of DeKalb and Flatbush Avenue Extension. This is where my grandfather decided to open his next Enduro Sandwich Shop. His bride-to-be, Ruth Jacobsen, wasn't so convinced, saying "Harry, what are you thinking?" Grandpa looked at her with a smile and replied, "If I listen to you, my darling, we'll be wearing cigar boxes for shoes."

In February of 1929, Grandpa Harry and Mike opened their Enduro in Brooklyn, in a small storefront rented from the Dime Savings Bank. It had only a few tables and a counter, but it soon became the place for Brooklynites to enjoy a steaming bowl of homemade tomato soup and a Jewish deli-style overstuffed sandwich: brisket of corned beef, roast beef, or hot turkey—take your pick. Business was good.

Ruth and Grandpa married and returned to Brooklyn from their honeymoon just as the stock market crashed. Grandpa Harry and Mike lost a lot of money (a couple of hundred thousand dollars, a major fortune in today's dollars), so they decided to sell their Manhattan shops and put all of their efforts into the Enduro in Brooklyn.

The Enduro Goes Upscale

In the early 1930s, Prohibition was repealed, which brought the breweries—and jobs—back to Brooklyn. This spurred Grandpa to expand, adding a cocktail bar and elevated bandstand, which turned his little luncheonette into the Enduro Restaurant and Café. The menu offered fine dining at its best: sirloin steaks, chops, side dishes like Duchess potatoes, and Enduro's parfait for dessert. By then, Grandpa had two sons—my Uncle Marvin, who was born in 1930, and my dad, Walter Rosen, born in 1934. Uncle Marvin began working at the restaurant in 1941, when he was eleven, and my dad in 1944, at age ten.

With the start of World War II, the Brooklyn Navy Yard was in full swing, and in 1943 Grandpa and Mike expanded the Enduro to an even larger space on the same corner, much like Junior's today, with a vertical Enduro marquee. But by 1949, the servicemen were gone, as were the crowds that fueled the Enduro's success. With the restaurant deep in debt, Mike decided to cut his losses and called it quits. But my grandmother challenged my grandfather to invent something new.

"All You Want. As You Want It."

In reinventing the Enduro, Grandpa took his inspiration from family-style restaurants that served breakfast, lunch, and dinner. This new Enduro menu would feature home-cooked meals and offer everything that Junior's is known for today—great breakfast, homemade soups, overstuffed deli sandwiches, and towering fountain desserts. Gone would be the nightclub look; in its place would be clean, sleek lines, light wood counters, modern-looking hanging lamps, and bright orange Naugahyde booths and chairs—the real '50s look. It would be warm and welcoming—a place you would want to come back to again and again.

But there was a problem. Grandpa was broke. With his new concept in hand, though, many friends offered to help, like Julie Palumbo, a contractor, who, on a handshake, agreed to supply materials and work on spec until the new restaurant was up and running. (Grandpa never forgot Julie!) But what to name this new restaurant? Grandpa decided to call it Junior's.

Junior's opened on Election Day, November 7, 1950—and a tradition began. Grandpa gave his customers what they came for—home-cooked food, impeccable service, and, most of all, his welcoming smile. And the folks kept on coming, from early morning until the wee small hours of the night. From creamy egg salad to fresh brisket on rye, they loved it all. Junior's was up and running!

Great Food Means Great Desserts

Grandpa knew that if Junior's was going to be a truly great restaurant, it had to have the best desserts around, so he hired Danish-born baker Eigel Peterson to turn out specialties for his new restaurant. The pair soon became a familiar sight in the bakery. Everywhere Grandpa went, he would bring back something he liked—a sweet bread one day, a three-layered devil's food cake the next, berry pie another day. Then he and Eigel would spend hours in the bakery not trying to replicate it but rather to make a version that was even better—what we call The Junior's Way today. Many of those first desserts are still on the menu, made using the very same recipes—fresh strawberry shortcake, cherry crumb pie, fresh strawberry cream cheese pie, and, of course, the Original New York Cheesecake, which didn't appear on the menu until the 1960s.

Brooklyn Changes and Junior's Stays

In the 1960s, there seemed to be tension everywhere, including Brooklyn: civil rights demonstrations, the Cold War got even colder, the Paramount and Fox theaters closed (the Albee held out until the mid-1970s). During the '60s, many businesses and Brooklynites left Brooklyn, but Junior's remained and became a destination restaurant, the main attraction on the corner of Flatbush Avenue Extension @ DeKalb.

In 1968, Uncle Marvin and my dad took over the day-to-day responsibilities of Junior's. Marvin's daughters, Sheri and Beth, and son, Jeffrey, as well as my brothers, Brett and Kevin, and myself all were born during these years. Three of our longest-tenured employees joined the business around this time: Camille Russo in 1960, Mary Blevins in 1962, and Fred Morgan in 1972. In the 1970s, Kevin and I started helping out at the restaurant—Kevin first helped Camille set the Danish on the bakery trays; then he joined me in doily-separation duty.

We're #1!

In July 1973, Ron Rosenbaum wrote in the *Village Voice*, "There will never be a better cheesecake than the cheesecake they serve at Junior's…it makes, as Carl Reiner and Mel Brooks once said, 'your mouth want to throw a party for your tongue.'" That fall, without us knowing it, *New York* magazine set out to find the best New York-style cheesecake. They rated twelve different cheesecakes for freshness, quality of ingredients, and taste. The judges unanimously chose Junior's cheesecake as the Champion Cheesecake of all cheesecakes in New York City. We even beat out the cakes from the famous Stage Deli and Ratner's. We had won the Cheesecake Olympics!

Upon hearing the news, we ordered orange "We're #1" buttons, and after the magazine hit the stands, our business doubled. By 1977, the bakers at Junior's were baking cheesecakes morning, noon, and night. Folks began arriving daily for a taste of our comfort food and a slice of our now world-famous cheesecake. New York politicians like mayors Abe Beame and Ed Koch made Junior's their "official" Brooklyn headquarters (this tradition has continued with mayors Dinkins, Giuliani, and Bloomberg). Then the celebrities came. We've had the privilege of serving Elvis Presley, Joe Torre, Robert DeNiro, Ron Howard, Nathan Lane, P. Diddy, Jay-Z, even Bill Clinton. But the real celebrities are you, our regular customers!

Save the Cheesecake!

Our story has not been all roses. At 1 a.m. on a hot August night in 1981, a fire broke out and destroyed Junior's. Luckily, all 50 employees and the 75 customers in the restaurant at the time got out safely. Firemen worked all night to extinguish the fire. And as they worked, onlookers chanted "Save the cheesecake! Save the cheesecake!" But in the end, there was little left of Junior's but ashes.

We started rebuilding right away. Our staff—from bakers to cooks to waiters—showed up, even though they knew they would be out of work for months. Everyone pitched in to save the cheesecake. We began almost immediately to bake our cakes using spare oven space in the old Barton Candy factory on DeKalb Avenue. We sold them as fast as we could bake them at our Cheese Cakerie, which we opened in the Albee Mall nearby. Day by day, cake by cake, we saved Junior's and our cheesecakes!

Nine months and three days later, Junior's reopened on May 27, 1982. It had the same Junior's look, but was bigger and better than ever: three floors and 27,000 square feet. There was room for 450 seats instead of 350, plenty of extra space for larger parties, a fully stocked bar, even a sidewalk café. We updated our kitchens and refurbished the bakery. Dignitaries came out for the opening. Borough President Howard Golden proclaimed the day "Junior's Day." Grandpa was there too, of course: thanking God, thanking Brooklyn, thanking everyone for coming. Customers came from near and far—they lined up from early in the morning until late at night for a slice of our cheesecake. No one seemed to mind waiting. It was just like Grandpa always said: "Give folks what they want, when they want it. If you do that, they will come." And that day, we found out they would wait for hours for a slice of Junior's cheesecake!

Junior's, Bigger and Better Than Ever!

I came home to Junior's in 1993 to join my brother Kevin, who had been working there full-time since 1988. Kevin and I, the third generation of Rosens, began making the day-to-day decisions of running the business. We continued to do a flourishing business in downtown Brooklyn, but also started selling cheesecakes through mail order.

In 1999, Mayor Rudy Giuliani dedicated the corner of Flatbush Avenue Extension @ DeKalb in honor of my Grandpa Harry, the event coinciding with the publication of our first cookbook, *Welcome to Junior's!*

In 2000, we opened Junior's in Grand Central Station in the heart of New York City. In 2006, we opened Junior's Times Square, on 45th Street @ Shubert Alley, between Broadway and 8th Avenue. Whether you're seeing a Broadway show or just out on the town, stop by for a nosh. We've brought the whole Brooklyn experience to Manhattan—in an uptown sort of way, complete with a spectacular dining spot.

Our newest restaurant is at the MGM Grand at Foxwoods, in Mashantucket, Connecticut. Enter right off the lobby and step into our grandest Junior's yet, with all the glamour and excitement of the Foxwoods Casino.

In 2007, we published our second book, *Junior's Cheesecake Cookbook,* by Beth Allen and me. As with the first book, we heard from readers all over the country about how excited they were to be able bake a Junior's cheesecake at home—and impress all of their friends!

Celebrate 60 Years with Us!

After 60 years, we decided it was time to write our third cookbook, to celebrate with you—our readers and friends—what we're all about…where we've been, what we've learned, how we've grown, what we've accomplished, and what makes us The Best. We wanted to pay homage to my grandfather Harry, my father Walter, and my uncle Marvin—for without them, there would not be a Junior's at all…it would not exist.

So we've gathered together a collection of our very favorite Junior's desserts. We've included recipes for our luscious lemon meringue pie (reimagined as individual tartlets), our mountain-high ice cream sundaes and triple-rich malteds, our famous fresh strawberry shortcake, decadent triple fudge brownies, and, of course, the cheesecake that made us famous, our Original New York Cheesecake, all adapted for the home kitchen. In addition, we developed some brand-new recipes just for this book, desserts you won't find on any of our Junior's menus or via mail order, like Boston Cream Pie and The Best Cheese Blintzes. We've also brought back desserts Junior's used to offer on its menu in the 1950s, when it first opened, like the delicious Banana Whipped Cream Pie.

We want to give a great big sweet thank you to all of our customers during these first 60 years—from our regulars who keep coming back and bringing their friends and family to our mail-order customers and visitors from other states and countries. And a sweet "hello" as well to those who are discovering Junior's for the first time. We promise that, at Junior's, you will always find great home-cooked food and great cheesecake, every day—all you want, as you want it, just as my Grandpa Harry promised! You are very important to us…for at Junior's, we care.

—Alan Rosen

Junior's Famous Cheesecakes

"Cheesecake has become part of our identity at Junior's — sometimes we think too much so, because our food is also delicious!" says Alan Rosen. But when you say "cheesecake" in New York, people say "Junior's!"

Grandpa Harry Rosen opened Junior's on Election Day, 1950, on the corner of Flatbush Avenue Extension @ DeKalb, where the Enduro Restaurant had operated since 1929 and where the original Junior's still stands today.

By the late 1950s, Junior's had become known as a great restaurant with generous portions, high-quality food, and delicious desserts — cakes, pies, breads, cookies. But something was missing. Grandpa Harry knew he had to have a fabulous cheesecake!

There were lots of competitors selling cheesecake in those days: Lindy's, Reuben's, The Brass Rail, even the local diner down the street. Everywhere he went, Grandpa Harry looked for cheesecakes to bring back to Eigel Peterson, his Danish-born baker. Together they would taste and sample the cakes and bake and bake, until finally they hit upon the magic formula and THE cheesecake came out of the oven — rich, creamy, and melt-in-your-mouth delicious, with luscious cream cheese flavor and a hint of lemon, supplied by its sponge-cake crust. The recipe for Junior's Original New York Cheesecake has not changed to this day.

It's been described by many as the best cheesecake in the world. "There will never be a better cheesecake than the cheesecake they serve at Junior's on Flatbush Avenue…it's the best cheesecake in New York," wrote Ron Rosenblum (Village Voice, July 26, 1973). That fall, a jury of six cool-headed cheesecake lovers for New York magazine named Junior's the Champion Cheesecake. Since that day, writers, celebrities, and just plain folks have tried to describe the deliciousness of Junior's cheesecake, using such words as smooth and light, soft and creamy, even heavenly. However you choose to say it, it's the quintessential, the original, New York cheesecake!

junior's original new york cheesecake

MAKES ONE 9- OR 8-INCH CHEESECAKE, ABOUT 2 ½ INCHES HIGH

FOR A 9-INCH CHEESECAKE

One 9-inch Sponge-Cake Crust (page 15), baked and cooled

Four 8-ounce packages Philadelphia® cream cheese (use only full fat), at room temperature

1 ⅔ cups sugar

¼ cup cornstarch

1 tablespoon pure vanilla extract

2 extra-large eggs

¾ cup heavy or whipping cream

(continued on page 14)

1. Make and bake the sponge-cake crust as the recipe directs. Let cool in the pan on a wire rack. Leave the oven on at 350°F.

2. While the sponge-cake crust cools, make the cheesecake filling. Place one package of the cream cheese, ⅓ cup of the sugar, and the cornstarch in a large bowl. Beat with an electric mixer (using the paddle attachment, if you have it) on low for about 3 minutes to make a stable starter batter. Blend in the remaining cream cheese, one package at a time, scraping down the bowl after adding each one. This will take about another 3 minutes.

3. Increase the mixer speed to medium (no faster!) and beat in the remaining sugar, then the vanilla. Blend in the eggs, one at a time, beating well after each one. Beat in the cream just until completely blended. The filling will look light, creamy, airy, and almost like billowy clouds. *Be careful not to overmix!* Gently spoon the filling over the crust.

4. Place the pan in the center of a large shallow pan containing hot water that comes about 1 inch up the side of the springform. Bake until the edge of the filling is light golden brown and the top is light golden tan, about 1¼ hours.

(continued on page 14)

FOR AN 8-INCH CAKE

One 8-inch Sponge-Cake Crust
(page 15), baked and cooled

Three 8-ounce packages
Philadelphia cream cheese
(use only full fat), at room
temperature

1⅓ cups sugar

3 tablespoons cornstarch

1 tablespoon pure vanilla extract

2 extra-large eggs

⅔ cup heavy or whipping cream

5. Gently remove the cake from the water bath, transfer it to a wire rack, remove the foil, and leave it on the rack (just walk away—don't move it) for at least 2 hours. The less you move it, the less likely it is your cake will crack. Once it has cooled, leave the cake in the pan, cover loosely with plastic wrap, and refrigerate overnight. Release and remove the side of the springform pan, leaving the cake on the bottom of the pan. Place on a serving plate.

6. If you wish to remove the cake from the bottom of the pan, freeze the cake in the pan for about 30 minutes, enough to firm it up. Warm the bottom by placing it on a hot wet towel or over a burner on very low heat for about 15 seconds—just long enough to melt the butter used to grease the pan but not long enough to make the pan hot. Release the spring and, using potholders, remove the side of the pan. Now, insert a long metal spatula between the cake and the pan bottom, move it in a circle, and lift up on the cake ever so gently, just enough to release the vacuum. Slide the cake onto a serving plate, using the spatula and your hands. Serve (see The Junior's Way, page 25, for how to cut a professional-looking piece of cheesecake); cover any leftover cake and refrigerate for up to 3 days or wrap and freeze for up to 1 month.

The Junior's Way

• Because Junior's cheescakes start with quality ingredients, they make every one with Philadelphia brand cream cheese. They always use the full-fat product, as low-fat cream cheese does not work when baking these cakes.

• Use two speeds of the electric mixer to mix the batter: slow to cream one package of cream cheese with a little sugar and the cornstarch, then medium to beat in the rest of the cream cheese, the eggs,

vanilla, and cream. Take your time, about 6 to 7 minutes total.

• Stop the mixer several times and scrape down the side of the bowl to ensure all the cream cheese is blended thoroughly and none collects at the bottom. This ensures that all of the ingredients are incorporated into the batter. Undissolved particles can result in undesirable air bubbles on the top of your cake.

• Always bake your cheesecake in a water bath. It evens out the heat,

keeps the cake moist and creamy, gives the cheesecake a smooth top, and protects against cracking. Watch the temperature of the water. If it begins to boil, it's too hot; add some cold water. Above all, don't let it boil dry, or the cake will not bake evenly.

• Be sure the temperature of your oven is 350°F. Buy an oven thermometer if you have any doubts. Overbaking will probably cause the top to crack; underbaking can cause it to fall in the center.

sponge-cake crust

FOR ONE 9-INCH SPONGE-CAKE CRUST

⅓ cup sifted cake flour

¾ teaspoon baking powder

Pinch of salt

2 extra-large eggs, separated

⅓ cup sugar

1 teaspoon pure vanilla extract

2 drops pure lemon extract

2 tablespoons unsalted butter, melted

¼ teaspoon cream of tartar

FOR ONE 8-INCH SPONGE-CAKE CRUST

¼ cup sifted cake flour

½ teaspoon baking powder

Pinch of salt

2 extra-large eggs, separated

¼ cup sugar

¾ teaspoon pure vanilla extract

2 drops pure lemon extract

2 tablespoons unsalted butter, melted

¼ teaspoon cream of tartar

1. Preheat the oven to 350°F. Generously butter the bottom and side of a 9- or 8-inch springform pan (preferably nonstick). Wrap the outside with aluminum foil, covering the bottom and extending all the way up the side, so water will not leak into the cheesecake as it bakes. Sift the flour, baking powder, and salt together, then place it back in the sifter.

2. Beat the egg yolks in a large bowl with an electric mixer on high for 3 minutes. With the mixer still running, slowly add half the sugar and continue beating until thick, light yellow ribbons form, about 5 minutes more. Beat in the extracts. Sift the flour mixture over the batter and stir with a wooden spoon just until no more white flecks appear—don't overmix! Blend in the melted butter. Wash the beaters of the mixer well and dry them.

3. Beat the egg whites and cream of tartar in a clean medium bowl with the mixer on high until frothy. Gradually add the remaining sugar and continue beating until stiff peaks form (the whites will stand up and look glossy but not dry). Fold about one-third of the whites into the batter, then the remaining whites. Don't worry if you still see a few white specks, as they'll disappear during baking.

4. Gently spread the batter over the bottom of the pan. Bake just until the top looks set and golden (not wet or sticky), about 10 minutes. Touch the cake gently in the center; when it springs back, it's done. Watch carefully and don't overbake (it should be golden, not browned). Place the pan on a wire rack to cool.

The Junior's Way

• Use cake flour, not all-purpose flour, and sift it before measuring. Also sift the flour, baking powder, and salt together. This disperses the ingredients throughout, ensuring that the cake rises evenly.

• Use only butter, not margarine.

• Beat the egg yolks until thick, light yellow ribbons form. Don't skimp on the beating time! This is the secret for baking a tender and light cake with an even grain with no large holes. If your mixer has a wire whip attachment, use it.

• Stir in the flour mixture with a wooden spoon. Using an electric mixer for this step can overdevelop the gluten and make the sponge cake tough.

Leave it to Junior's to create a tiramisu dessert like no other. It starts with their sponge-cake crust, which they flavor with a little espresso, as they also do the cheesecake batter. After baking, it's topped with a heavenly mixture of whipped cream and mascarpone, the decadent Italian triple-cream cheese. The side of the cake is edged with delicate ladyfingers and the top gets a fine dusting of dark cocoa—what a showstopper! This cake deserves a ribbon—so two very talented and skilled Junior's personnel on the cake-finishing line tie a bright red bow around each cake, just before placing it into a Junior's box.

tiramisu charlotte

MAKES ONE 9-INCH CHEESECAKE, ABOUT 3 INCHES HIGH

FOR THE SPONGE-CAKE CRUST

One 9-inch Junior's Sponge-Cake Crust (page 15), baked

2 tablespoons instant espresso powder

2 tablespoons water

FOR THE CHEESECAKE FILLING

Three 8-ounce packages Philadelphia cream cheese (use only full fat), at room temperature

1⅓ cups granulated sugar

3 tablespoons cornstarch

1 tablespoon pure vanilla extract

2 extra-large eggs

1 tablespoon instant espresso powder

1 tablespoon water

⅔ cup heavy or whipping cream

(continued on page 18)

1. Make and bake the sponge-cake crust. Let cool in the pan on a wire rack. Dissolve the espresso in the water and sprinkle over the crust in the pan. Let soak while making the cheesecake filling. Leave the oven on at 350°F.

2. Make the cheesecake filling. Place one package of the cream cheese, ⅓ cup of the granulated sugar, and the cornstarch in a large bowl. Beat with an electric mixer (using the paddle attachment, if you have it) on low for about 3 minutes to make a stable starter batter. Blend in the remaining cream cheese, one package at a time, scraping down the bowl after each one. This will take about another 3 minutes.

3. Increase the mixer speed to medium (no faster!) and beat in the remaining 1 cup granulated sugar, then the vanilla. Blend in the eggs, one at a time, beating well after each one. Dissolve the instant espresso in the water and stir into the cream. Beat the cream into the batter, just until completely blended. The filling will look light, creamy, airy, and almost like billowy clouds. *Be careful not to overmix!* Gently spoon the filling over the crust.

4. Place the springform pan in the center of a large shallow pan containing hot water that comes about 1 inch up the side of the springform. Bake until the edge of the filling is light golden brown and the top is light golden tan, about 1¼ hours.

(continued on page 18)

tiramisu charlotte (continued)

FOR THE MASCARPONE CREAM

3 tablespoons confectioners' sugar

1 teaspoon cream of tartar

1 pint (2 cups) icy-cold heavy or whipping cream

1 tablespoon pure vanilla extract

One 8- to 10-ounce carton mascarpone cheese

FOR DECORATING THE CAKE

13 to 14 ladyfingers, split lengthwise into 26 to 28 halves

Confectioners' sugar for dusting (about ¼ cup)

1 tablespoon unsweetened dark cocoa powder (100% cacao)

1 teaspoon granulated sugar

Red satin ribbon, 60 inches long, ½ inch wide

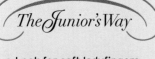

The Junior's Way

• Look for soft ladyfingers (not the crispy Italian ones) in the fresh fruit section of the supermarket.

• You need 13 to 14 lady-fingers, split in half length-wise to ring the cake. (Count before you buy—you may need to purchase two packages.)

• Do not separate the ladyfingers, but spread the cut sides with a little mascarpone and stand them up around the cake.

5. Gently remove the cake from the water bath, transfer it to a wire rack, remove the foil, and let it cool for 2 hours (just walk away—don't move it). Once cooled, cover loosely with plastic wrap and refrigerate until completely cold, preferably overnight or for at least 4 hours.

6. After the cake is cold, make the mascarpone cream. Mix the confectioners' sugar and cream of tartar together. Whip the cream in a medium bowl with the electric mixer on high just until it begins to thicken. With the mixer running, add the confectioners' sugar mixture, then the vanilla, and continue beating until the cream stands up in stiff (but still flowing) peaks. Don't overbeat or the cream will curdle. Gently fold in the mascarpone cheese with a rubber spatula. Remove 1 cup of the cream and refrigerate (you will need it to attach the lady-fingers to the side of the cake). Spoon the remaining mascarpone cream on top of the chilled cake in the pan. Cover the pan with plastic wrap and place in the freezer; freeze solid, about 2 hours (or overnight if you wish).

7. Release and remove the cake from the pan and onto a cake plate (see The Junior's Way, page 25). To ring the cake with the ladyfingers, first lightly dust the rounded sides of the ladyfingers with the confectioners' sugar. Spread a thin layer of the reserved mascarpone cream over the cut sides of the lady-fingers. Now attach them to the side of the cake: Working with a group of 6 ladyfingers at a time, stand them up around the edge of the cake, rounded sides out, pressing each one gently in place. Mix the cocoa with the granulated sugar and lightly sprinkle on top of the cake. Tie the ribbon around the cake and refrigerate until ready to serve. If the cake is still frozen when you wish to serve, let it stand at room temperature for about 30 minutes or until easy to cut. Slice with a sharp straight-edge slicing knife, not a serrated cake knife. Cover any leftover cake and refrigerate for up to 3 days or wrap and freeze for up to 1 month.

This was the Grand Prize Winner of the Junior's 60th Anniversary Cheesecake Contest, submitted by Suzanne Banfield of Basking Ridge, New Jersey. Suzanne was born in Brooklyn and loved going to Junior's while growing up. She jumped at the chance to compete in Junior's cheesecake bake-off and developed this recipe in honor of her favorite candy bar.

joyful almond cheesecake

MAKES ONE 9-INCH CHEESECAKE, 2½ INCHES HIGH

FOR THE ALMOND SPONGE-CAKE CRUST

⅓ cup cake flour

¾ teaspoon baking powder

2 extra-large eggs, separated

5 tablespoons sugar

½ teaspoon pure almond extract

2 tablespoons unsalted butter, melted

¼ teaspoon fresh lemon juice

¼ cup finely chopped blanched almonds

¼ cup sweetened shredded or angel-flake coconut

FOR THE COCONUT CREAM CHEESECAKE FILLING

Four 8-ounce packages Philadelphia cream cheese (use only full fat), at room temperature

1 cup sugar

¼ cup cornstarch

1 teaspoon pure vanilla extract

¾ teaspoon pure coconut extract

2 extra-large eggs

¾ cup canned cream of coconut

(continued on page 21)

1. Preheat the oven to 350°F. Generously butter the bottom and side of a 9-inch springform pan (preferably nonstick) with softened (not melted) butter. Wrap the outside of the pan with heavy-duty aluminum foil, covering the bottom and extending all the way up the side.

2. Make the almond sponge-cake crust. Whisk the flour and baking powder together in a small bowl. Beat the egg yolks in a large bowl with an electric mixer on high for 3 minutes. With the mixer still running, add 2 tablespoons of the sugar and the almond extract. Continue beating until thick, light yellow ribbons form, about 5 minutes more. Sprinkle the flour mixture over the egg yolks and stir with a wooden spoon just until all the white specks disappear— don't overmix! Blend in the melted butter. Wash the beaters well and dry.

3. Beat the egg whites and lemon juice in a clean medium bowl with the mixer on high until frothy. Gradually add the remaining 3 tablespoons sugar and continue beating until glossy peaks form. Fold about one-third of the whites into the batter, then the remaining whites. Fold in the chopped almonds.

4. Gently spread the batter over the bottom of the prepared pan and sprinkle with the coconut. Bake just until the top looks set and golden and it springs back when lightly touched in the center, about 12 minutes. (Watch carefully and don't overbake.) Let the crust cool in the pan on a wire rack while you prepare the cheesecake filling. Leave the oven on at 350°F.

(continued on page 21)

joyful almond cheesecake (continued)

FOR THE TOPPING

1 cup Chocolate Ganache
(pages 128-129)

¼ to 1 cup coarsely chopped
blanched almonds (depending
on the width of the border
you wish)

The Junior's Way

On November 2, 2010,
hundreds of folks came
to Junior's flagship store
in Brooklyn to celebrate
Junior's 60th anniversary
with a 60-cent slice of
cheesecake. While people
were lining up outside,
the National Cheesecake
Contest bake-off was in
full swing inside. Suzanne
Banfield took home first-
place honors and $1,800
for this recipe.

5. Make the coconut cream cheesecake filling. Place one package of the cream cheese, ⅓ cup of the sugar, and the cornstarch in a large bowl. With an electric mixer (using the paddle attachment, if you have it) on low, beat for about 3 minutes. Blend in the remaining cream cheese, one package at a time, scraping down the bowl after each one. This will take about another 3 minutes.

6. Increase the mixer speed to medium (no faster!) and beat in the remaining ⅔ cup sugar, then the vanilla and coconut extracts. Blend in the eggs, one at a time, beating well after each one. Beat in the cream of coconut just until completely blended. The filling will look light and creamy. *Be careful not to overmix!* Gently spoon the filling over the crust.

7. Place the springform pan in the center of a large shallow pan containing hot water that comes about 1 inch up the side of the springform. Bake until the edge of the filling is light golden brown and firm, the top is light golden tan, and the center still has a little jiggle, about 1¼ hours.

8. Gently remove the cake from the water bath, transfer it to a wire rack, remove the foil, and let it cool for 2 hours (just walk away—don't move it). Once it has cooled, leave the cake in the pan, cover loosely with plastic wrap, and refrigerate until completely cold, preferably overnight or for at least 4 hours. Release and remove the side of the springform pan, leaving the cake on the bottom of the pan. Place on a serving plate.

9. Make the ganache. Frost the side and top of the cheesecake, smoothing the ganache evenly with a narrow, long icing spatula (work quickly!). To finish, use the spatula to make even ridges by dragging it across the top, from side to side, about 1 inch apart. Sprinkle the almonds around the outside edge, making a 1½- to 2-inch border on the top (you will need about 1 cup almonds for this width of border). Refrigerate the cake for at least 1 hour to set the ganache before serving. Slice with a sharp straight-edge slicing knife, not a serrated cake knife. Cover any leftover cake and refrigerate for up to 1 week or wrap and freeze for up to 1 month.

When Valentine's Day rolls around, you start to see hundreds—make that thousands—of heart-shaped cheesecakes coming out of the bake ovens at Junior's and into the refrigerators to chill. Next, they are showered with chocolate ganache, covered with bittersweet chocolate chips, then decorated with thin pinstripes of red frosting. Each is placed into an orange-and-white striped box and packed safely for travel to one of Junior's restaurants, bakery stores, or thousands of lucky recipients all over the world. What a perfect way to say, "Be mine, the Junior's way!" You'll need a heart-shaped nonstick baking pan, preferably springform, that measures 9 inches wide, 9½ inches long, and 2¾ inches high to make this valentine.

"be mine" valentine cheesecake

FOR THE SPONGE-CAKE CRUST
Batter for one 9-inch Junior's Sponge-Cake Crust (page 15)

FOR THE CHEESECAKE FILLING
Four 8-ounce packages Philadelphia cream cheese (use only full fat), at room temperature

1⅔ cups granulated sugar

¼ cup cornstarch

1 tablespoon pure vanilla extract

2 extra-large eggs

¾ cup heavy or whipping cream

(continued on page 24)

MAKES ONE 9-INCH HEART-SHAPED CHEESECAKE, ABOUT 2½ INCHES HIGH

1. Preheat the oven to 350°F. Generously butter the bottom and sides of a 10-cup heart-shaped pan (about 9 inches wide, 9½ inches long, 2¾ inches high), preferably nonstick and springform, with softened (not melted) butter. If you are using a springform pan, wrap the outside with heavy-duty aluminum foil, covering the bottom and extending all the way up the side. If not a springform, line the pan with two pieces of aluminum foil, crisscrossing them and leaving a 3-inch overhang all around. Press the foil gently, smoothly, and firmly into the pan, being careful not to tear the foil. There's no need to wrap the outside of this pan. Butter the foil well.

2. Pour the batter for the sponge-cake crust into the prepared pan and bake as directed. Remove the pan from the oven and set on a wire rack to cool. Leave the oven on at 350°F.

3. While the sponge-cake crust cools, make the cheesecake filling. Place one package of the cream cheese, ⅓ cup of the granulated sugar, and the cornstarch in a large bowl. Beat with an electric mixer (using the paddle attachment, if you

(continued on page 24)

FOR THE DECORATION

2 cups Chocolate Ganache
(pages 128-129)

2 cups Nestlé® Toll House®
chocolate morsels (regular size
chips)

**FOR THE BUTTERCREAM PIPING
(MAKES 3 CUPS)**

3 cups sifted confectioners' sugar
(¾ pound)

¼ teaspoon salt

¾ cup (1½ sticks) unsalted butter,
at room temperature (important!)

3 tablespoons vegetable
shortening

2 teaspoons light corn syrup

2 teaspoons pure vanilla extract

2 teaspoons fresh lemon juice

2 to 3 tablespoons cold heavy or
whipping cream

Red food coloring (preferably
icing gel)

have it) on low for about 3 minutes to make a stable starter batter. Blend in the remaining cream cheese, one package at a time, scraping down the bowl after each one. This will take about another 3 minutes.

4. Increase the mixer speed to medium (no faster!) and beat in the remaining 1⅓ cups granulated sugar, then the vanilla. Blend in the eggs, one at a time, beating well after each one. Beat in the cream just until completely blended. The filling will look light, creamy, airy, and almost like billowy clouds. *Be careful not to overmix!* Gently spoon the filling over the crust.

5. Place the cake pan in the center of a large shallow pan containing hot water that comes about 1 inch up the sides of the cake pan. Bake until the edges of the filling are light golden brown and the top is light golden tan, about 1¼ hours.

6. Gently remove the cake pan from the water bath, transfer it to a wire rack, remove the foil (if using a springform pan), and let it cool for 2 hours (just walk away—don't move it). Once cooled, cover loosely with plastic wrap and refrigerate until completely cold, preferably overnight or for at least 4 hours. Freeze the cake for 1 hour before removing from the pan.

7. Release and remove the cake from the pan if in a springform pan. If using a non-springform pan, place the pan directly on a hot, wet towel to melt the butter used to grease the pan. Place a cake plate or rimless platter on top of the pan and invert both of them. If the cake does not release easily from the pan, see The Junior's Way, opposite. Gently peel away the foil.

8. Make the ganache, then frost the top and sides of the cake, smoothing the ganache evenly (work quickly!). Cover the sides with the chocolate chips, angling them in different directions.

9. Make the buttercream. Sift the confectioners' sugar and salt together. In a large bowl with an electric mixer on high, beat the butter and shortening together until creamy, about 3 minutes, scraping down the bowl once or twice. While the mixer is running, beat in the corn syrup, vanilla, and lemon juice. Reduce the speed to low and add the confectioners' sugar in 2 additions. Add 2 tablespoons of the cream and beat on high until light, airy, almost fluffy, about 3 minutes. Add a little more cream, 1 teaspoon at a time as needed, to reach spreading consistency. Color the buttercream a dark red like they do at Junior's;

it should be almost burgundy-red. To pipe the pinstripes, fit a pastry bag with a small round tip (#1, #2, or #3) and fill three-fourths full with the buttercream. Pipe thin, dark red vertical lines from the top to the bottom of the heart.

10. Refrigerate the cake for at least 1 hour to set the ganache before serving. Slice with a sharp straight-edge slicing knife, not a serrated cake knife. Cover any leftover cake and refrigerate for up to 3 days or wrap and freeze for up to 1 month.

The Junior's Way

- Here's a tip for removing a cheesecake from the bottom of the springform pan. First, put it in the freezer until it firms up, at least 30 minutes. Then warm the bottom of the pan by placing it directly on a hot wet towel or over a burner turned to very low heat for about 15 seconds (use potholders!), just long enough to melt the butter used to grease the pan but not so long as to make the pan hot. Slowly release the spring and, with the potholders, remove the ring of the pan. Insert a long metal spatula between the cake and the bottom of the pan and, moving it in a circle, lift up the cake ever so gently. Quickly slide the cake onto a serving plate, using the spatula and your hands.

- Before icing it with ganache, place the cake in the freezer for 30 minutes. This helps the icing stay right where you want it while you're frosting.

- Use a long spatula to smooth the ganache evenly on the top to give it a professional look. It is especially important to have a flat surface before piping on the pinstripes. An offset-handled icing spatula works particularly well. Work quickly, as the ganache sets up fast on the cold cake.

- A small frosting tip will give you thin red lines that look like pinstripes. Make them an equal distance apart and as even as you can pipe them!

- If you would rather not make your own buttercream for the pinstripes, look in your supermarket or a cake decorating shop for a tube of ready-to-use dark red decorator's icing. Buy the darkest red one—and the smallest round tip that fits onto the tube—that you can find.

- To cut a professional looking slice of cheesecake, be sure the cake is chilled. Use a straight-edge slicer knife, with a long thin narrow blade—not a serrated cake knife. Hold the knife under hot running water until it's hot, then wipe it dry and make the first cut. After making each cut, and before making the next, wipe the knife with a wet hot towel and dry it. Slice down and do not "saw" the cake as you cut.

Fabulous Soda Fountain Desserts

Nothing says "Junior's" like one of their sodas, shakes, sundaes, or egg creams. Each is over the top in every way! Junior's New York egg creams are offered up in four different flavors, each topped with a thick layer of white foam, just the way it should be. Their famous Broadway Skyscraper Ice Cream Soda comes to you still bubbling, with a double giant scoop of coffee ice cream hanging off the rim of the glass and crowned with a huge mound of whipped cream and a cherry. The Orange Freeze is deliciously whirled up with fresh orange juice and about a pint of orange sherbet, and their banana split is served up with three flavors of ice cream, each topped with a different sauce. These and Junior's other soda fountain specialties are always sensational. Try the recipes and make them yourself, the Junior's Way!

"My grandfather Harry Rosen—Grandpa Harry to me—was only 16 when he was already running his own soda shop in lower Manhattan with his brother Mike. It was a luncheonette where they made pretzels and egg creams. That small restaurant grew into several Enduro Sandwich Shops and was the beginning of what Junior's is today. Egg creams are at the base of our business—it's where our roots are, it's how Junior's began," declares Alan Rosen.

"There has always been a big debate over what goes in first—the syrup or the milk. In Brooklyn, it's the syrup; in the Bronx, it's the milk. Obviously, at Junior's we follow the Brooklyn way and start with the syrup."

You only need Fox's u-bet® syrup, milk, and seltzer to make a perfect Junior's egg cream. No egg, no cream—but a lot of Junior's know-how. The secret is using the freshest ingredients in the correct proportions and knowing when and how to stir them. As the foam starts to form, begin stirring quickly and vigorously, until a thick foam reaches the top of the glass. "It should be white foam—not the color of mud," explains Alan.

junior's egg creams

chocolate egg cream

MAKES ONE 16-OUNCE EGG CREAM

¼ cup Fox's u-bet or other top-quality chocolate syrup

⅓ cup icy-cold whole milk

¾ to 1 cup icy-cold sparkling seltzer (fresh and bubbly!)

1. Pour the syrup into a tall 16-ounce glass.

2. Pour in the milk, but don't stir.

3. Quickly pour in the seltzer over the back of a long-handled spoon, letting it bubble and bounce off the spoon. Keep pouring and stirring vigorously until a thick white foam rises to the top. Serve immediately before the foam starts to settle and disappear.

(continued on page 30)

junior's egg creams (continued)

COFFEE EGG CREAM

For each egg cream, you need: ¼ cup Fox's u-bet coffee syrup, ⅓ cup icy-cold whole milk, and ¾ to 1 cup icy-cold seltzer.

STRAWBERRY EGG CREAM

For each egg cream, you need: ¼ cup Fox's u-bet strawberry syrup, ⅓ cup icy-cold whole milk, and ¾ to 1 cup icy-cold seltzer.

VANILLA EGG CREAM

For each egg cream, you need: ¼ cup Fox's u-bet vanilla syrup, ⅓ cup icy-cold whole milk, and ¾ to 1 cup icy-cold seltzer.

The Junior's Way

- If you can't find Fox's u-bet syrups in your supermarket, buy them online or buy another quality brand. You can also try the Italian syrups used to flavor coffee.

- Make sure the milk is icy cold and very fresh. Junior's only uses *whole* milk in their egg creams because the higher the fat content, the better the flavor.

- Be sure the seltzer is also icy cold, very fresh (preferably just opened), and bubbly. Also, "If you have a SodaStream™ maker, use it. Seltzer from one of these home soda-maker machines makes a great egg cream!" advises Alan.

- You need a long-handled spoon for the stirring—an iced-tea spoon is perfect.

- Once the thick white foam starts rising to the top of the egg cream, run with it to the table—fast! You want to enjoy your egg cream before the foam settles.

- Junior's special egg cream glass makes it all very easy. Just follow the lines: syrup up to the first line, milk to the second line, then stir in the seltzer until white foam bubbles to the top. The glass is available at Junior's or online, but you can use any tall 16-ounce glass.

"Once you've mastered mixing up a Junior's egg cream," explains Alan Rosen, "making an ice cream soda, the Junior's way, is easy. It's really an egg cream with a double giant scoop of ice cream perched on the rim of the glass. That's all there is to it." That, plus a couple of tall peaks of freshly whipped cream on top (be sure not to cover up the ice cream), making each soda "as high as a skyscraper." Finish it all off with a bright red cherry.

junior's skyscraper ice cream sodas

broadway skyscraper ice cream soda

MAKES 1 GIANT ICE CREAM SODA

¼ cup Fox's u-bet or other top-quality chocolate syrup

⅓ cup icy-cold whole milk

¾ to 1 cup icy-cold seltzer (fresh and bubbly!)

2 giant scoops coffee ice cream (about ¾ pint)

About 1 cup Decorator's Never-Fail Whipped Cream (pages 130-131)

1 red maraschino cherry with a stem

1. Pour the syrup into a tall 16-ounce glass.

2. Pour in the milk, but don't stir.

3. Quickly pour in some of the seltzer over the back of a long-handled iced-tea spoon. Keep pouring and stirring vigorously until a thick white foam of bubbles rises to the top.

4. Take a giant scoop of ice cream, one that's overflowing out of the scoop, and hang it securely over the rim of the glass. Make a second scoop, a little smaller and slightly flat on one side. Perch the flat side gently on top of the first scoop, making a tall double-scoop that hangs down from the rim.

5. Pipe (using a pastry bag with a large closed-star tip) or swirl the whipped cream on top of the soda, piping as high as you like to make a small mountain—going higher and higher while leaving the ice cream showing. Crown with the cherry and serve immediately.

COFFEE SKYSCRAPER ICE CREAM SODA

For each ice cream soda, you need: ¼ cup Fox's u-bet coffee syrup, ⅓ cup icy-cold whole milk, ¾ to 1 cup icy-cold seltzer, 2 giant scoops coffee ice cream

(continued on page 32)

The Junior's Way

• Make sure the ice cream is frozen hard; let it thaw just enough so you can scoop it out into solid balls of ice cream. Don't worry if a little of the ice cream falls into the soda. It will just make it extra creamy.

• Be sure the milk and seltzer are both icy cold, and serve the ice cream soda fast, before the white foam of seltzer bubbles begins to settle.

• H. Fox & Co. doesn't make a pineapple syrup (needed to make the Hoboken) but Torani® (available in the Italian section of your supermarket or online) does. You can also use pineapple ice cream topping (sold in most supermarkets) instead, which gives you the added benefit of a few delicious pineapple chunks in the bottom of your glass.

(about ¾ pint), about 1 cup Decorator's Never-Fail Whipped Cream (pages 130–131), and 1 red maraschino cherry with a stem.

THE HOBOKEN ICE CREAM SODA

"The combination of a pineapple ice cream soda with coffee ice cream may sound odd, but it tastes delicious," says Alan.

For each ice cream soda, you need: ¼ cup pineapple syrup, ⅓ cup icy-cold whole milk, ¾ to 1 cup icy-cold seltzer, 2 giant scoops coffee ice cream (about ¾ pint), about 1 cup Decorator's Never-Fail Whipped Cream (pages 130–131), and 1 red maraschino cherry with a stem.

STRAWBERRY SKYSCRAPER ICE CREAM SODA

For each ice cream soda, you need: ¼ cup Fox's u-bet strawberry syrup, ⅓ cup icy-cold whole milk, ¾ to 1 cup icy-cold seltzer, 2 giant scoops strawberry ice cream (about ¾ pint), about 1 cup Decorator's Never-Fail Whipped Cream (pages 130–131), and 1 red maraschino cherry with a stem.

VANILLA SKYSCRAPER ICE CREAM SODA

For each ice cream soda, you need: ¼ cup Fox's u-bet vanilla syrup, ⅓ cup icy-cold whole milk, ¾ to 1 cup icy-cold seltzer, 2 giant scoops vanilla ice cream (about ¾ pint), about 1 cup Decorator's Never-Fail Whipped Cream (pages 130–131), and 1 red maraschino cherry with a stem.

You can rely on Junior's to take a plain Cherry Coke® and turn it into a soda-fountain masterpiece! A little ice cream syrup, some ice-cold Coke, one of their famous giant scoops of ice cream, and plenty of whipped cream…that's all it takes. But don't expect Junior's to float the ice cream in the soda like everyone else does. They perch it right on the rim of the glass for all to see.

junior's cherry coke float

MAKES 1 TALL COKE FLOAT

¼ cup Fox's u-bet or other top-quality black cherry syrup

12 ounces ice-cold Coca-Cola® (1½ cups)

2 giant scoops vanilla ice cream (about ¾ pint)

About 1 cup Decorator's Never-Fail Whipped Cream (pages 130–131)

1 red maraschino cherry with a stem

1. Pour the syrup into a tall 16-ounce soda glass. Vigorously stir in the cola until well blended, giving the drink a slightly rosy color.

2. Take a giant scoop of ice cream, one that's overflowing the scoop, and hang it securely over the rim of the glass. Make a second scoop that's a little smaller than the first. Perch it gently on top, making a tall double-scoop that hangs down from the rim.

3. Pipe (using a pastry bag with a large closed-star tip) or swirl the whipped cream, counterclockwise, on top of the float, piping as high as you like to make a small mountain—going higher and higher while leaving the ice cream showing. Crown with the cherry and serve immediately.

The Junior's Way

• Junior's uses Fox's u-bet black cherry syrup, usually found at the supermarket with the ice cream toppings; also check the syrups used for flavoring coffee in the Italian section. Or you can order it online.

• Junior's uses very cold, highly carbonated soda right out of the soda machine for their Coke floats. In fact, the soda might be bubbling over the side of the glass a little when it arrives at your table. For the best results at home, use a just-opened bottle or can of cola.

• Be sure the ice cream is frozen hard; let it thaw just enough so you can scoop it out into solid balls of ice cream that are firm enough to hang over the rim of the glass.

It takes only four ingredients to make a Junior's Orange Freeze: orange sherbet, orange juice, whipped cream, and a cherry. But WOW, what a treat it is! Also, it's a terrific way to get kids to drink their orange juice. There's a whole cup of juice in every drink.

junior's orange freeze

3 giant scoops orange sherbet (about 1 pint)

1 cup fresh orange juice

About 1 cup Decorator's Never-Fail Whipped Cream (pages 130–131)

1 red maraschino cherry with a stem

1. Place 2 scoops of the orange sherbet and all of the orange juice in a blender. Whirl on high for 1 to 2 minutes, until all of the sherbet is incorporated into the drink and blended throughout. The freeze will be thick, creamy, and slushy—and just thin enough to sip through a straw. Pour into a tall 16-ounce glass.

2. Hang the last giant scoop of sherbet over the rim of the glass. If you have extra sherbet, make a smaller scoop and perch it on top, making a huge double scoop that hangs down from the rim.

3. Pipe (using a pastry bag with a large closed-star tip) or swirl the whipped cream on top of the freeze, piping as high as you like to make a small mountain—going higher and higher while still leaving the sherbet showing. Crown with the cherry and serve immediately.

The Junior's Way

Use sherbet—*not* sorbet (sherbet contains milk, sorbet doesn't), for a creamier freeze. Be sure the sherbet is frozen solid.

It's the truth—Junior's makes the creamiest, richest, most heavenly milk shakes you've ever tasted! What's the secret? Maybe it's the u-bet syrups they flavor them with, made just a stone's throw away from the restaurant in the Bronxville section of Brooklyn by the Fox family since the 1920s. Or it could be the top-quality ice cream they use. Or perhaps it's the mixology know-how, handed down for several generations, beginning with Grandpa Harry in his Manhattan soda shoppe in the early 1930s. Whatever the reason, a Junior's milk shake is certainly worth the trip.

junior's milk shakes with ice cream

chocolate milk shake with ice cream

MAKES ONE 1 TALL SHAKE

3 giant scoops chocolate ice cream (about 1 pint)

¾ cup icy-cold whole milk

¼ cup Fox's u-bet or other top-quality chocolate syrup

About 1½ cups Decorator's Never-Fail Whipped Cream (pages 130–131)

1 red maraschino cherry with a stem

1. Put the ice cream, milk, and syrup in the blender in that order.

2. Whirl on high for 1 to 2 minutes, until thick and smooth. Pour into a tall 16-ounce soda glass.

3. Starting at the outside rim of the glass, pipe (using a pastry bag with a large closed-star tip) or swirl the whipped cream around and around, counterclockwise, going higher and higher, until you reach the center and a mountain of cream covers the entire top of the milk shake. Top with the cherry.

BANANA MILK SHAKE WITH ICE CREAM

For each shake, add to the blender in this order: 3 giant scoops vanilla ice cream (about 1 pint), ¾ cup icy-cold whole milk, and 1 large ripe banana, peeled and cut into ½-inch-thick rounds. Whirl until smooth, then top with about 1½ cups Decorator's Never-Fail Whipped Cream (pages 130–131) and 1 red maraschino cherry with a stem.

STRAWBERRY MILK SHAKE WITH ICE CREAM

For each shake, add to the blender in this order: 3 giant scoops strawberry ice cream (about 1 pint), ¾ cup icy-cold whole milk, and ¼ cup Fox's u-bet strawberry syrup. Whirl until smooth, then top with about 1½ cups Decorator's Never-Fail Whipped Cream (pages 130–131) and 1 red maraschino cherry with a stem.

The Junior's Way

• Buy the richest, best ice cream you can find. Junior's only uses top-quality Schrafft's. And if it's vanilla, it's vanilla bean.

• Use only the freshest milk—whole, not low fat or skim. Be sure it's icy cold.

• The syrup is the last ingredient to go into the blender to keep it from getting trapped in the blades on the bottom when the machine is turned on.

When you're served a sundae at Junior's, it arrives in an oversize sundae glass on a pedestal that shimmers and sparkles like fine crystal. Regardless of which flavor you order, every sundae comes topped with a mountain of whipped cream and is always crowned with a red cherry on top. That's why Junior's calls them Mountain-High Sundaes. You'll find swirls and layers of thick sundae sauce or syrup, especially after the ice cream softens just a bit, making every bite richer than the last.

junior's mountain-high sundaes

strawberry mountain-high sundae

MAKES 1 LARGE SUNDAE

Generous ¾ cup Junior's Fresh Strawberry Sauce (page 140)

2 giant scoops strawberry ice cream (about ¾ pint)

About 1½ cups Decorator's Never-Fail Whipped Cream (pages 130–131)

1 tablespoon slivered blanched almonds

1 red maraschino cherry with a stem

1. Drizzle one-third of the berry sauce in the bottom of a large (12-ounce) glass sundae dish (preferably one with a pedestal). Place a giant scoop of ice cream on top.

2. Drizzle the ice cream with half the remaining berry sauce. Add the other giant scoop of ice cream. Cover with the remaining berry sauce.

3. Starting at the outside rim of the sundae glass, pipe (using a pastry bag fitted with a closed-star tip) or swirl the whipped cream around and around, counterclockwise, going higher and higher, until you reach the center and a mountain of cream covers the entire top of the sundae. Sprinkle with the slivered almonds and crown with the cherry.

COFFEE MOUNTAIN-HIGH SUNDAE

For each sundae, you need: generous ¾ cup Fox's u-bet coffee syrup, 2 giant scoops vanilla ice cream (about ¾ pint), 1½ cups Decorator's Never-Fail Whipped Cream (pages 130–131), 1 tablespoon slivered almonds, and 1 red maraschino cherry with a stem.

The Junior's Way If your grocer does not carry Fox's u-bet coffee syrup, order it online. Or look in the Italian section of your supermarket for the flavored syrups used for making coffee drinks.

HOT BUTTERSCOTCH MOUNTAIN-HIGH SUNDAE

For each sundae, you need: generous ¾ cup warm store-bought butterscotch ice cream topping, 2 giant scoops vanilla ice cream (about ¾ pint), about 1½ cups Decorator's Never-Fail Whipped Cream (pages 130–131), 1 tablespoon slivered almonds, and 1 red maraschino cherry with a stem.

The Junior's Way You won't find a butterscotch sundae on the menu at Junior's, but it's a soda fountain favorite for many people, so we included this one "in the style of Junior's."

FRESH BLUEBERRY MOUNTAIN-HIGH BLUEBERRY SUNDAE

For each sundae, you need: generous ¾ cup blueberry syrup, 2 giant scoops vanilla ice cream (about ¾ pint), ⅓ cup fresh blueberries, about 1½ cups Decorator's Never-Fail Whipped Cream (pages 130–131), 1 tablespoon slivered almonds, and 1 red maraschino cherry with a stem.

The Junior's Way H. Fox & Co. doesn't make a blueberry syrup, but you can find it from other companies where the pancake syrup is sold in the supermarket.

To build this sundae, begin with one-third of the syrup, top with a giant scoop of the ice cream, cover with half the remaining syrup, and sprinkle on half of the blueberries. Add the second giant scoop of ice cream, drizzle with the remaining syrup, and sprinkle with the remaining berries. Crown with the whipped cream, sprinkle with the almonds, and top with the cherry.

CHOCOLATE-MARSHMALLOW MOUNTAIN-HIGH SUNDAE

For each sundae, you need: generous ¾ cup Fox's u-bet chocolate syrup, 2 giant scoops vanilla ice cream (about ¾ pint), ½ cup Marshmallow Fluff®, about 1½ cups Decorator's Never-Fail Whipped Cream (pages 130–131), 1 tablespoon slivered almonds, and 1 red maraschino cherry with a stem.

The Junior's Way To build this sundae, start with one-third of the chocolate syrup, top with a giant scoop of the ice cream, drizzle with half the remaining chocolate syrup, and spoon on half the Marshmallow Fluff. Add the second giant scoop of ice cream, drizzle with the remaining syrup, and top with the remaining Fluff. Crown with the whipped cream, sprinkle with the almonds, and top with the cherry.

Order a banana split at Junior's and you're in for a surprise. All you see at first is a big glass dish covered in whipped cream and topped with slivered almonds and a cherry. What's underneath are the old-fashioned traditional ingredients: a whole banana plus three giant scoops of ice cream, each topped with a different sauce. Dig in—and good luck eating the whole thing!

junior's banana split

MAKES 1 BIG BANANA SPLIT, SERVING 1 VERY GENEROUSLY

1 large banana, peeled and split lengthwise

1 giant scoop chocolate ice cream (about ¾ cup)

1 giant scoop strawberry ice cream (about ¾ cup)

1 giant scoop vanilla ice cream (about ¾ cup)

¼ cup Junior's Fresh Strawberry Sauce (page 140)

¼ cup pineapple ice cream topping (look for it in the ice cream topping section of the supermarket)

1 recipe The Best! Fudge Sauce (page 139) or store-bought (you'll need ¼ cup, plus extra for drizzling on top), warmed

About 1½ cups Decorator's Never-Fail Whipped Cream (pages 130–131)

2 tablespoons slivered almonds

1 red maraschino cherry with a stem

1. Place the banana halves, cut side up, in the bottom of a large dessert bowl, preferably a clear glass one. Scoop in the 3 ice creams, placing them in a row along the entire length of the banana.

2. Top the chocolate ice cream with the strawberry sauce, the strawberry ice cream with the pineapple topping, and the vanilla ice cream with the hot fudge.

3. Starting at the outside rim of the dessert bowl, pipe (using a pastry bag fitted with a closed-star tip) or swirl the whipped cream around and around, counterclockwise, going higher and higher, until you reach the center and a mountain of whipped cream covers the entire top of the banana split. Drizzle extra hot fudge sauce over the sundae and sprinkle with the almonds. Finish it off with the cherry.

The Junior's Way

Use at least ¼ cup of each of the toppings— or even a little more if you like. More is definitely better at Junior's!

Black & Whites

"Part of the charm of Junior's is that it is all about New York," explains Alan Rosen. "Especially New York in the 1950s, which is when Grandpa Harry opened Junior's. We're still using many of the same recipes. Then, as now, Junior's menu featured food that New Yorkers love to eat. And black and white foods are high on their list! It first began with our Black & White Malted, which led to the Black & White Cookie, which has now evolved into our Miracle Cupcakes and our Marble Loaf. Black and white is everywhere at Junior's!"

You won't find these Oreo® Little Fellas at Junior's...at least not yet. But you will find plenty of other Little Fellas—in Junior's bakery in Grand Central Station, in the "bakery on Broadway" inside their restaurant in Shubert Alley, in the MGM Grand at Foxwoods, and, of course, in their flagship restaurant in Brooklyn. There's nothing little about the popularity of Junior's Little Fellas!

oreo little fellas

FOR THE OREO CRUMB COOKIE CRUST AND COOKIE BITS

One 16.6-ounce package full-size Oreo sandwich cookies with filling

⅓ cup sugar

½ cup (1 stick) unsalted butter, melted

FOR THE CHEESECAKE FILLING

Three 8-ounce packages Philadelphia cream cheese (use only full fat), at room temperature

1⅓ cups sugar

3 tablespoons cornstarch

1 tablespoon pure vanilla extract

2 extra-large eggs

⅔ cup heavy or whipping cream

FOR THE FROSTING AND DECORATION

11 cups Junior's Cream Cheese Frosting (pages 137-138)

24 mini Oreo bite-size cookies (one-third of an 8-ounce package)

MAKES 2 DOZEN LITTLE FELLAS

1. Preheat the oven to 350°F. Line 24 standard muffin cups (2¾ inches in diameter) with silicone, paper, foil, or parchment liners.

2. Separate the full-size cookies (you should have 82 to 84 chocolate cookies). Scrape off and discard the filling. Break up 30 of the cookies into ¼-inch bits (you will have about 1½ cups of cookie bits); set aside.

3. Pulse the remaining unbroken cookies in a food processor until fine crumbs form. Add the sugar and process 1 minute to mix. You will have about 2 cups of cookie crumbs. With the processor running, slowly add the melted butter through the feed tube and process until the crumbs are moistened and come together. Press about 1 tablespoon of crumbs into the bottom of each muffin cup liner.

4. Make the cheesecake filling. In a large bowl with an electric mixer (using the paddle attachment if you have it) on low, beat one package of the cream cheese, ⅓ cup of the sugar, and the cornstarch together for about 3 minutes to make a stable starter batter. Beat in the remaining cream cheese, one package at a time, scraping down the bowl after each one. This will take about another 3 minutes.

5. Increase the mixer speed to medium (no faster) and beat in the remaining 1 cup sugar, then the vanilla. Blend in the eggs, one at a time, beating well after each one. Beat in the cream just until completely blended. The filling will look light, creamy, airy, and almost like billowy clouds. *(Be careful not to overmix!)*

(continued on page 46)

6. Fill the muffin cups with 2 heaping spoonfuls of batter (it should come very close to the top of the liners). Drop 6 to 8 of the small cookie bits on top of the batter in each muffin cup. Use a small spoon to gently push the bits down into the batter, just until you can no longer see them (be careful not to push all the way to the bottom).

7. Place the muffin tins in a large shallow pan, then add enough hot water so it comes about 1 inch up the sides of the tins. Bake the cakes until they are set and the centers are golden, 45 to 50 minutes. Transfer the muffin tins to a wire rack and let cool for 2 hours. Cover the cakes with plastic wrap (do not remove from the tin) and freeze until cold and set, about 1 hour.

8. If you baked the cakes in reusable silicone liners, remove them from the liners before serving (they pop right out). If using paper or foil liners, it's fine to leave them on for serving.

9. Make the cream cheese frosting. Fit a pastry bag with a medium open-star (#1M or #822) or closed-star tip (#35 or #844) and pack it about three-fourths full with the frosting. Starting at the outside of the cakes, pipe sweeping "ruffles" on top in one direction, swirling higher and higher into the center until the tops of the cakes are completely covered. Finish the center off with one last swirl, higher than the rest. Crown each with a mini Oreo. Arrange on a serving platter and refrigerate until time to serve. Store any leftover cakes in the refrigerator or wrap and freeze (see The Junior's Way, below) for up to 1 month.

The Junior's Way

• If both muffin tins don't fit in the water bath, don't worry. Refrigerate the second tin and bake it after the first batch.

• Not sure you can eat all 2 dozen Little Fellas in the next few days? Freeze the extras. Fill, bake, and frost them as the recipe directs, but

don't top them with the mini Oreos. Stand the Little Fellas up straight, uncovered, on a tray and place in the freezer. Once they have frozen solid, slide them into a zip-top freezer bag. To serve, defrost as many as you wish by letting them stand at room temperature for an hour, then decorate each with a mini Oreo.

• For the ultimate finishing touch, if you have extra Oreo bits left, crush them finely. Pipe an extra ring of frosting around the outside edge of each cake. Push the edge of the icing down slightly over the edge with your thumbs and sprinkle the crumbs around the outside edge of each Little Fella.

Marble cake is always on the menu at Junior's. Called Marble Loaf, it's two cakes in one: a rich, golden butter cake swirled and baked with a deep dark chocolate one. This is one loaf cake that is oh-so-easy to slice and even easier to eat. It's a breakfast cake, an afternoon snacking cake, and an after-dinner dessert—whatever suits your appetite. This recipe makes two loaves, but the loaf freezes beautifully.

marble loaf

3⅓ cups sifted cake flour

1 tablespoon baking powder

1 teaspoon salt

1½ cups (3 sticks) unsalted butter, at room temperature

2½ cups sugar

6 extra-large eggs, separated

1½ tablespoons pure vanilla extract

1 cup heavy or whipping cream

¼ teaspoon cream of tartar

6 ounces bittersweet chocolate (at least 60% cacao), melted

¼ teaspoon baking soda

MAKES TWO 1½-POUND LOAVES (10 X 5 X 3 INCHES) OR THREE 1-POUND LOAVES (8½ X 4½ X 2¾ INCHES)

1. Preheat the oven to 350°F. Generously butter the bottoms and sides of two 1½-pound loaf pans (10 x 5 x 3 inches) or three 1-pound loaf pans (8½ x 4½ x 2¾ inches), preferably nonstick. Line the bottoms only with parchment paper. Sift together the flour, baking powder, and salt, then place it back in the sifter.

2. In a large bowl with an electric mixer on high, cream the butter and sugar together until light yellow and creamy. Add the egg yolks, one at a time, beating well after each one. Beat in the vanilla. Sift about one-third of the flour mixture over the batter and stir in with a wooden spoon, then stir in about one-third of the cream. Repeat until both have been incorporated. Wash the mixer beaters well and dry them.

3. In a large bowl with the mixer on high, beat the egg whites and cream of tartar until stiff but not dry peaks form. Using a rubber spatula, fold about one-third of the whites into the cake batter until they disappear, then gently fold in the remaining whites. Don't worry if you still see a few white specks— they'll disappear during baking. Transfer half the batter to another bowl.

4. In a small bowl, mix together the melted chocolate and baking soda. Stir this into one bowl of batter, mixing until completely blended. You now have two bowls of batter: one chocolate and one vanilla. If making 2 loaves, spoon one-fourth of the vanilla batter over the bottom of each of the prepared pans and spread it out evenly (you will have half of the vanilla batter left). Top each

(continued on page 49)

loaf with half the chocolate batter, using it all, and spread it out evenly. Top each loaf with half the remaining vanilla batter, using it all up. If making 3 loaves, spread one-sixth of the vanilla batter over the bottom of each of the pans and top each with one-third of the chocolate batter, using it all up and spreading it evenly over the vanilla batter. Top each loaf with one-third of the remaining vanilla batter, using it all up.

5. Holding a large spoon slightly at an angle and starting at one end of the pan, dip the spoon down to the bottom and bring it back up, swirling the vanilla and chocolate batters together. Work down to the other end of the pan, creating figure 8s of white and chocolate batter as you go. (Once you reach the other end of the loaf, stop swirling, or you're likely to end up with an all-chocolate loaf.)

6. Bake until set and a pick inserted in the centers comes out with moist crumbs, 50 to 55 minutes. Turn off the oven and let the loaves rest inside the oven with the door closed for 10 minutes (this allows the centers to firm up). Remove from the oven and cool the loaves in the pans on wire racks for 15 minutes. Turn the loaves out onto the racks and remove the parchment liners. These loaves are great warm or at room temperature. Try toasting a slice for breakfast! The loaf freezes well, either whole or cut into 1-inch-thick slices, for up to 1 month. Wrap in plastic wrap and slip into a zip-top plastic freezer bag.

The Junior's Way

- When swirling the chocolate and vanilla batters in the pans, use a large spoon, like a serving spoon. Don't swirl too much or you'll end up with a chocolate loaf instead of the wonderful marbled effect you want.

- You can use the microwave to melt chocolate instead of doing it on the stovetop. If you choose this method, be sure to check the chocolate frequently as it melts. Place the chocolate in a microwave-safe bowl for 1 minute at first, then stir and continue to microwave and stir until the chocolate is almost melted (some little pieces should still be visible). Remove and stir until completely melted and smooth.

"One of our friend's sons gave these little cakes their name," explains Alan. "First we bake our devil's food cupcakes. Then each one gets a generous coating of rich chocolate ganache and a corkscrew of white buttercream on top." Go ahead and take a bite and discover the "miracle" for yourself—more yummy buttercream is hidden inside!

miracle cupcakes

2¾ cups sifted all-purpose flour

1 tablespoon baking powder

1 teaspoon salt

½ teaspoon baking soda

1 cup (2 sticks) unsalted butter, at room temperature

1⅓ cups granulated sugar

⅓ cup firmly packed light brown sugar

3 extra-large eggs

6 ounces bittersweet chocolate (at least 60% cacao), melted

1 tablespoon unsulfured molasses (mild-flavored, not robust or blackstrap)

1 tablespoon pure vanilla extract

¾ cup whole milk (not low fat or nonfat)

10 cups Decorator's Buttercream (pages 132–134)

3 cups Chocolate Ganache (pages 128–129)

MAKES 24 FILLED CUPCAKES

1. Preheat the oven to 350°F. Line 24 standard muffin cups (2¾ inches in diameter) with paper, foil, or parchment liners. Sift the flour, baking powder, salt, and baking soda together in a small bowl.

2. In a large bowl with an electric mixer (using the paddle attachment if you have it) on medium, cream the butter and both sugars together until light and creamy. Add the eggs, one at a time, beating after each one. Beat in the melted chocolate, molasses, and vanilla. Using a wooden spoon, stir in some of the flour mixture, then some of the milk. Repeat until both have been incorporated.

3. Fill the muffin cups almost to the tops of the liners (about seven-eighths full). Bake until set and a pick inserted in the centers comes out with moist crumbs, about 25 minutes. Cool in the tins on a wire rack for 15 minutes, then lift out of the tins with a small spatula and onto the rack to cool completely before filling and frosting.

4. Make the buttercream. Fit a pastry bag with a coupler and a medium open-star tip (see The Junior's Way, page 51) and fill the bag three-fourths full with the frosting. Press the tip from the top about two-thirds of the way down into the center of each of the cooled cupcakes (don't go all the way through). Squeeze the bag, filling each cupcake with about 1 tablespoon of buttercream (squeeze until the frosting reaches the top of the cupcake). Wipe the tip clean with a damp paper towel between cupcakes *(important!)*. Brush away any crumbs from the tops.

5. Make the ganache, transfer it into a small, deep heatproof bowl, and cool in the freezer just until it thickens, 10 to 15 minutes. Dip and swirl the top of each cupcake in the ganache and set it, top side up, on a wire rack. Repeat until all the cupcakes are frosted.

6. Change the decorating tip on the pastry bag to a small round tip (such as a #4 or #5). Decorate the top of each cupcake with a corkscrew design. Let stand for at least an hour before serving. These are best served the day they are made, but can be wrapped individually in plastic and frozen for up to 1 month.

The Junior's Way

• Use a pastry bag to fill each cupcake. The medium open-star tip (#1M or #822) does the job best. The small points on the star tip make it easy to insert it inside the cupcake.

• Be sure to use a coupler to attach the tip. It holds the tip firmly in place as you work. Piping without a coupler can result in the cake pushing the tip back inside the bag without filling the cupcake.

• Before frosting with the ganache, check each cupcake. If any white buttercream appears, use a small spatula to lift it off; brush away any crumbs. The top and edges need to be perfectly clean before icing these cakes.

These cookies are a staple at Junior's. No one seems to know exactly who baked the first one, or where. But we do know Black & Whites can be found in delis, coffee shops, bakeries, and restaurants all around the five boroughs of New York City, and now throughout the country. They sometimes go by other names—Half-Moon Cookies or Half-and-Half Cookies—but whatever they're called, they're the same. Buttery, soft, large round cookies that are more cake-like then cookie-like. They are iced half "white" (vanilla) and half "black" (chocolate). And the unique feature: you ice these cookies on their bottoms, not on their tops!

black & white cookies

FOR THE COOKIES

2½ cups sifted cake flour

2 cups sifted all-purpose flour

2 teaspoons baking powder

2 teaspoons salt

1½ cups (3 sticks) unsalted butter, at room temperature

2 cups granulated sugar

4 extra-large eggs

1 tablespoon pure vanilla extract

1 teaspoon pure lemon extract

⅔ cup heavy or whipping cream

(continued on page 54)

MAKES ABOUT 25 FOUR-INCH COOKIES

1. Preheat the oven to 375°F. Line 2 baking sheets with parchment paper, securing it to the pans with a dab of butter. Sift both the flours, the baking powder, and salt together, then place the mixture back in the sifter.

2. In a large bowl with an electric mixer (using the paddle attachment if you have it) on medium, cream the butter and granulated sugar together until light yellow and creamy. Add the eggs, one at a time, beating well after each one. Beat in the extracts. Sift about one-third of the flour mixture over the batter and, using a wooden spoon, stir it in, then add about one-third of the cream and stir until mixed. Repeat until both are incorporated.

3. Using a ¼-cup measure, scoop about ¼ cup batter onto the prepared baking sheets for each cookie. Spread out with a small metal spatula into a 3-inch circle. Space the cookies about 3 inches apart (you will be able to fit only about 6 cookies on an 18 x 16-inch baking sheet).

4. Bake just until the edges begin to turn light golden and the tops are puffed and spring back when touched, 12 to 13 minutes. The cookies should be only light golden on the bottom, not golden brown. A pick inserted into the center should come out clean. *(Do not overbake!)* Let the baked cookies cool for 5 minutes on the baking sheets, then transfer, upside down (bottom side up),

(continued on page 54)

black & white cookies (continued)

FOR THE 2 FROSTINGS

10 cups sifted confectioners' sugar (2¹/₄ pounds)

¹/₂ cup light corn syrup

3 tablespoons fresh lemon juice

1¹/₂ tablespoons pure vanilla extract

¹/₂ cup plus 3 tablespoons hot water, plus more as needed

5 ounces bittersweet chocolate (at least 60% cacao), melted

to wire racks and cool completely while you bake the remaining cookies and make the frostings. Don't stack the cookies on top of one another, as they may stick together.

5. To make the frostings, place the confectioners' sugar in a medium bowl. Stir in the corn syrup, lemon juice, vanilla, and ¹/₂ cup hot water until smooth. Add more hot water, if needed, a little at a time, until the frosting is spreadable. Transfer 1¹/₄ cups frosting to another bowl; stir in the melted chocolate and the 3 tablespoons hot water. You will have two bowls of frosting: one vanilla and one chocolate. Cover the frostings with a damp paper towel to keep them fresh and spreadable as you work; if the frostings stiffen too much, stir in a few more drops of hot water.

6. Using a small metal spatula, preferably an offset one, spread white frosting over the entire flat bottom side of each cookie. When the frosting feels set, frost half of each cookie a second time, this time with chocolate frosting, layering it on top of the white and making the center line as straight as possible. Let the icing dry until it is no longer soft to the touch, at least 2 hours, and store the cookies, between sheets of parchment or waxed paper, in an airtight container at room temperature for up to 4 days. Do not refrigerate or freeze these cookies.

The Junior's Way

• Don't just drop these cookies onto the cookie sheet—spread each out into a 3-inch circle. This way they will bake up even, round, and smooth.

• Watch the cookies closely and take them out when they are just golden on the edges and light golden underneath.

• Bring the oven temperature back to 375°F after every batch. If the oven has lost too much heat, the cookies will take longer to bake and end up drying out.

• Here's an icing tip from Alan: "Frost the entire top of each cookie with white frosting, let it dry and set, then frost one-half again with the chocolate frosting. This makes it easier to get that straight, even line down the center and gives the cookies a more professional look."

Though you won't find this pie on the Junior's menu (at least not yet), here's another way to team up "Black & White." Chocolate ice cream, coffee ice cream, and chocolate wafer crumbs are layered inside a dark chocolate crumb crust, then decorated with chocolate ganache and lots of white whipped cream to make it fancy enough for any party. The best part? You can make it several days ahead. Or make two at a time and keep an extra one in the freezer for unexpected guests. Decorate it when you're ready to serve.

junior's mud pie

MAKES ONE 8- OR 9-INCH DEEP-DISH ICE CREAM PIE, ABOUT 6 INCHES HIGH

1 recipe Famous Chocolate Crumb Crust (page 124)

4 quarts (1 gallon) coffee ice cream

25 Nabisco® Famous® Chocolate Wafers

1 quart chocolate ice cream

4 cups Chocolate Ganache (pages 128-129)

6 cups Decorator's Never-Fail Whipped Cream (pages 130-131)

1. Make the crumb crust and press into a well-buttered 8- or 9-inch pie plate that can go into the freezer. Place in the freezer for at least 15 minutes to set.

2. Meanwhile, take 1 quart of the coffee ice cream out of the freezer and let soften just enough so it spreads but still holds it shape, about 15 minutes. Break the wafers into coarse crumbs (you need 1½ cups of crumbs).

3. Assemble the pie. First, work through the coffee ice cream with a rubber spatula to smooth out any lumps. To make the first layer, spread the softened ice cream in the crumb crust. Sprinkle with half the wafer crumbs, making a thin chocolate-crumb layer. Freeze until firm, about 1 hour.

4. Take the chocolate ice cream out of the freezer and let soften just enough so it spreads but still holds it shape, about 15 minutes. Work through it with the spatula. Spread evenly over the chocolate-crumb layer, then cover with the rest of the crumbs. Return to the freezer until set, about 1 hour.

5. Take 1½ quarts of the remaining coffee ice cream out of the freezer and let soften just enough so it spreads, about 15 minutes, then work through it with the spatula. Spread it over the top of the pie, above the rim of the pie plate, mounding it in the center (it will look slightly domed on top at this stage). Return the pie to the freezer until set and firm, about 1 hour.

(continued on page 56)

junior's mud pie (continued)

6. Let the remaining 1½ quarts coffee ice cream soften, then mound it very high in the center of the pie, the Junior's Way! The pie should be about 6 inches high in the center. Place in the freezer until very firm and solid to the touch, at least 3 hours or overnight.

7. When ready to decorate and serve the pie, prepare the ganache and place in the freezer to thicken slightly. Make the whipped cream. Starting at the center of the pie, slowly pour the cooled ganache in a circular motion, thickly covering the entire pie. The ganache should be about ¼ inch thick and will set up very quickly when it hits the frozen pie. Quickly repeat if some areas are not covered, reserving ½ cup for decorating.

8. Fit a pastry bag with a medium open-star tip (such as #1M or #822), fill it three-fourths full with the whipped cream, and pipe a border of rosettes around the edge of the pie. Using a small spoon with a pointed tip, drizzle the rest of the ganache over the rosettes. Return the pie to the freezer for at least 30 minutes or until time to serve. Let the pie stand at room temperature for about 15 minutes to make it easier to slice. Keep any leftover pie in the freezer and serve within 1 week.

The Junior's Way

• Break, don't cut or smash, the cookies, as they will shatter.

• Use plenty of ice cream and mound it high in the center to give the pie that Junior's over-the-top look (very impressive!).

• When slicing this pie, use a slicing knife with a long, thin blade (not a serrated one) to get the cleanest, most professional slices. Hold it under hot running water to warm it, then dry with a paper towel before cutting each new slice (very important!).

Junior's malteds are simply the creamiest, thanks to over a pint of ice cream that's swirled into each one. They use unflavored malted milk powder, which you can find at gourmet food stores or order online.

junior's black & white malted

MAKES 1 TALL MALTED

2 giant scoops chocolate ice cream (about ¾ pint)

1 giant scoop vanilla ice cream (about ¾ cup)

¾ cup icy-cold whole milk

¼ cup Fox's u-bet or other top-quality chocolate syrup

¼ cup unflavored malted milk powder

1 cup Decorator's Never-Fail Whipped Cream (pages 130–131)

1 red maraschino cherry with a stem

1. Put the first 5 ingredients in the blender in this order: both ice creams, milk, syrup, and malted milk powder.

2. Whirl on high just for 1 minute, until thick and smooth. Pour into a tall 16-ounce soda glass.

3. Starting at the outside rim of the glass, pipe (using a pastry bag fitted with a large closed-star tip) or swirl the whipped cream around and around, counter-clockwise, going higher and higher, until you reach the center and a mountain of cream covers the entire top of the malted. Top with the cherry and serve with a sipping straw, the Junior's way!

The Junior's Way

When mixing a malted or milk shake in your blender, process for only 1 minute *(no longer!)* to keep it nice and thick. Overblending can cause the malted to lose its thickness. The reason is simple: as you run the blender, its motor can heat up and melt the ice cream.

Junior's Layer Cakes & Cupcakes

Junior's customers know they must save room for dessert, as they have known ever since Grandpa Harry Rosen opened his first soda shoppe in the early 1920s, then operated the Enduro in the late 1920s, through the 1930s and '40s, and finally established Junior's in 1950. Today they're still serving fabulous desserts, many from those first early days, like their fresh berry shortcake. Folks also come for Junior's Coconut 4-Layer Cake and their rich Red Velvet 4-Layer Cake. And often diners leave with a signature orange-and-white-striped Junior's to-go box packed with their delicious cupcakes, swirled high with buttercream.

The second most popular dessert at Junior's is their Famous Fresh Strawberry Shortcake, which they've been serving 20 years longer than they have their cheesecake—it was on their menu when they opened in 1950. Here we've given it a delicious twist—making it with three kinds of berries instead of one.

junior's famous fresh 3-berry shortcake

MAKES ONE 9-INCH 4-LAYER CAKE, ABOUT 5 INCHES HIGH

FOR THE CAKE LAYERS

1⅓ cups sifted cake flour

1 tablespoon baking powder

½ teaspoon salt

9 extra-large eggs, separated

1⅓ cups sugar

1 tablespoon pure vanilla extract

½ teaspoon pure lemon extract

½ cup (1 stick) unsalted butter, melted

½ teaspoon cream of tartar

(continued on page 62)

1. Place a rack in the middle position in your oven and preheat to 350°F. Generously butter the bottoms and sides of two 9-inch round cake pans with 2-inch-high sides (preferably nonstick). Line the bottoms only with parchment paper. Sift together the flour, baking powder, and salt, then place it back into the sifter.

2. In a large bowl with an electric mixer on high, beat the yolks for 3 minutes. With the mixer running, slowly add half the sugar; continue beating until thick, light yellow ribbons form, about 5 minutes more. Beat in the extracts. Sift the flour mixture over the batter and stir in with a wooden spoon, just until no white flecks appear—don't overmix! Blend in the butter. Wash the beaters well and dry.

3. In another large bowl, beat the egg whites and cream of tartar with the mixer on high until frothy. Gradually add the rest of the sugar and continue beating until stiff peaks form (the whites will stand up and look glossy but not dry). Fold about one-third of the whites into the batter, then the remaining whites. Don't worry if you still see a few white specks, as they'll disappear during baking.

4. Divide the batter evenly between the 2 prepared cake pans and bake on the middle oven rack until the tops look set and golden (not wet or sticky) and a pick inserted in the centers comes out with moist crumbs clinging to it, about 25 minutes. Touch the cakes gently in the center. When they spring back, they are done. Watch carefully and don't let the tops brown. Transfer to wire racks and let cool in the pans for 15 minutes. Remove the cakes from the pans and let cool completely on the racks. Peel off the parchment liners.

(continued on page 62)

junior's famous fresh 3-berry shortcake (continued)

FOR THE FROSTING AND BERRY DECORATION

2 quarts ripe fresh strawberries

4 half-pints fresh raspberries (about 3 cups)

3 half-pints fresh blueberries (about 3 cups)

8 cups Decorator's Never-Fail Whipped Cream (pages 130–131)

FOR SERVING (OPTIONAL)

1 recipe Junior's Fresh Strawberry Sauce (page 140)

The Junior's Way

"Don't freeze this cake," advises Alan Rosen. "It will not look pretty or hold up when defrosted. The fruits will lose their shape, their colors will bleed, and the whipped cream frosting will lose its design."

5. Rinse and hull the strawberries, then dry on paper towels. Pick out 12 of the prettiest ones and set aside for decorating the top. Slice the remaining strawberries across into circles to use between the layers (you need about 4 cups). Rinse the raspberries and dry on paper towels. Pick out 12 of the prettiest ones and set aside. Rinse the blueberries and dry on paper towels. Pick out 25 of the prettiest ones and set aside. Cover the berries with a wet paper towel. Prepare the whipped cream, cover with a damp paper towel, and chill.

6. When the cakes have cooled completely, with a serrated knife cut each layer horizontally (with a sawing motion) into 2 equal layers—for a total of 4 thin layers. Brush away any crumbs. Place one layer, bottom side down, on a cake plate and spread with ½-inch-thick layer (about 1 cup) of the whipped cream. Scatter some sliced strawberries, raspberries, and blueberries over the top, pushing them down into the cream (this will help the layers stay together as you slice and serve this tall cake). Spread ⅓ cup cream over the top of the second layer and place, cream side down, on the first layer. Repeat in the same way with whipped cream and berries on top. Spread ⅓ cup cream over the top of the third layer and place, cream side down, on the second layer. Repeat with another ½-inch layer of cream and the remaining berries (excluding the reserved berries for the top). Spread ⅓ cup cream over the top of the fourth layer and place, cream side down, on the third layer. Fill in any empty spaces between the layers with whipped cream to even up the side. Brush away any crumbs. Refrigerate until chilled and set, 1 to 2 hours. Refrigerate the remaining whipped cream.

7. Frost the side and the top of the cake with whipped cream, using a ½- to ¾-inch layer of cream on the top. (Be sure to reserve some to pipe rosettes.) Use an icing spatula to smooth the side and top. Stand up a ring of whole strawberries about 1½ inches from the edge, then arrange a circle of raspberries in the center. Fill up the space between the two rings of raspberries with blueberries. Fit a pastry bag with a large open-star tip (#172 or #2110/1M), fill it three-fourths full with the remaining whipped cream, and pipe a border of whipped cream rosettes on the top, around the outside rim of the cake.

8. Refrigerate the cake for at least 1 hour or until serving time (but not more than 3 hours). In the meantime, prepare the strawberry sauce if using. Slice the cake with a sharp straight-edge slicing knife, not a serrated cake knife. This cake is best served the day it is made.

This cake is a sensation. It's based on the traditional recipe using cocoa but substitutes rich cream for the buttermilk found in some versions. It's all sandwiched together with Junior's oh-so-creamy, oh-so-delicious cream cheese frosting and stands 4 inches tall!

red velvet 4-layer cake

MAKES ONE 9-INCH 4-LAYER CAKE, ABOUT 4 INCHES HIGH

FOR THE CAKE

2½ cups sifted cake flour

1 tablespoon plus 1 teaspoon unsweetened dark cocoa powder (100% cacao)

2 teaspoons baking powder

½ teaspoon baking soda

½ teaspoon salt

1 cup heavy or whipping cream

2 tablespoons (1 ounce) liquid red food coloring

1 cup (2 sticks) unsalted butter, at room temperature

1½ cups sugar

3 extra-large eggs, separated

1 tablespoon unsulfured molasses (mild-flavored, not robust or blackstrap)

¼ cup vegetable oil

1 tablespoon pure vanilla extract

½ teaspoon cream of tartar

FOR THE FROSTING

11 cups Junior's Cream Cheese Frosting (pages 137-138)

1. Preheat the oven to 350°F. Generously butter the bottoms and sides of two 9-inch round cake pans with sides at least 2 inches high (preferably nonstick). Line the bottoms only with parchment paper (don't let the paper come up the sides). Sift together the flour, cocoa, baking powder, baking soda, and salt, then place the mixture back in the sifter.

2. Mix the cream and red food coloring together; set aside. In a large bowl with an electric mixer (using the paddle attachment if you have it) on medium, cream the butter and sugar together until light yellow and creamy. Add the egg yolks, one at a time, beating well after each one. Beat in the molasses. Beat in the oil and vanilla. Sift about one-third of the flour mixture over the batter and stir in with a wooden spoon, then stir in about one-third of the cream; repeat until all is incorporated. Wash the mixer beaters well and dry them.

3. In a medium bowl with the mixer on high, beat the egg whites and cream of tartar until stiff, but not dry, peaks form. Using a rubber spatula, fold about one-third of the whites into the cake batter until they disappear, then gently fold in the remaining whites. Don't worry if you still see a few white specks, as they'll disappear during baking. Divide the batter evenly between the 2 prepared cake pans and gently spread evenly over the bottom.

4. Bake until a pick inserted in the centers comes out with moist crumbs clinging to it, about 35 minutes. Transfer to wire racks and let cool in the pans for 15 minutes. Remove the layers from the pans and let cool on the racks completely. Peel off the parchment liners.

(continued on page 65)

5. After the cakes have cooled, using a serrated knife, cut a ½- to ¾-inch-thick slice from the tops of both layers, leveling them. Turn these slices into Decorator Cake Crumbs (page 127).

6. Make the cream cheese frosting. Place a damp paper towel directly on the surface of the frosting to keep it fresh and leave at room temperature.

7. Using a serrated knife, cut each layer in half horizontally (using a sawing motion), making 4 layers. Brush away any crumbs. Place one layer, bottom side down, on a cake plate and spread with ½-inch-thick layer of the frosting. Repeat with 2 more layers and more frosting. Top with the final cake layer, bottom side up. Fill in any empty spaces between the layers with frosting. Brush away any crumbs from the side and top of the cake layers (very important!). Place in the freezer or refrigerator until chilled and set, 1 to 2 hours. Cover the bowl of remaining frosting and refrigerate.

8. Frost the side and top of the cake, spreading the frosting over the top about ½ to ¾ inch deep. (Remember to reserve some frosting for the top decoration.) Using a long metal spatula that has been warmed under hot running water (then dried), smooth out the frosting on the side and top of the cake. Turn the spatula on its side, or use the tip of a boning knife, and run it across the cake in lines, 1 inch apart, cutting into the icing to make decorative ridges (be careful not to cut into the cake).

9. Using your hands, gently press the cake crumbs against the side of the cake, stopping at the top edge. Fit a pastry bag with a large open-star tip (such as a #172 or #4B), fill the bag with the remaining frosting, and twist tightly to close. Pipe swirls of frosting in an up-and-down design around the top outside rim of the cake. Slice the cake with a sharp straight-edge slicing knife, not a serrated cake knife. Cover any leftover cake and refrigerate for up to 3 days or wrap and freeze for up to 2 weeks.

This coconut cake is a variation on the one you'll find on the Junior's menu and in their bakery, using toasted coconut instead of fresh. More than 5 inches tall, it's a showstopper! Coconut is folded into the cake batter, as well as sprinkled between the finished cake layers, over the top, and on the sides. It's guaranteed to turn any occasion into a party!

toasted coconut 4-layer cake

MAKES ONE 9-INCH 4-LAYER CAKE, ABOUT 5 INCHES HIGH

FOR THE COCONUT CAKE LAYERS

Two 14-ounce packages sweetened angel-flake coconut

1 1/3 cups sifted cake flour

1 tablespoon baking powder

1/2 teaspoon salt

9 extra-large eggs, separated

1 1/3 cups sugar

1 tablespoon pure vanilla extract

2 teaspoons pure coconut extract

1/2 cup (1 stick) unsalted butter, melted

1/2 teaspoon cream of tartar

FOR THE FROSTING

12 cups Decorator's Buttercream (pages 132–134), adding 1 teaspoon pure coconut extract in step 2 with the vanilla extract

1. Preheat the oven to 350°F. Generously butter the bottoms and sides of two 9-inch round cake pans with sides 2 inches high (preferably nonstick). Line the bottoms only with parchment paper. Spread the coconut over a rimmed baking sheet and toast, tossing it 2 or 3 times, until it turns golden, 20 to 25 minutes. Watch carefully. Turn off the oven and let the coconut remain for 10 to 15 minutes to dry it out and give it a little more golden color. You will need about 8 cups. (If you do not use all of it, store the remainder in a zip-top plastic bag and use later for sprinkling over ice cream or pudding.)

2. Meanwhile, sift the flour, baking powder, and salt together, then place the mixture back in the sifter. In a large bowl with an electric mixer on high, beat the egg yolks for 3 minutes. While the mixer is still running, slowly add half the sugar and continue beating until thick, light yellow ribbons form, about 5 minutes more. Beat in the extracts. Sift the flour mixture over the batter and stir in with a wooden spoon, just until no more white flecks appear (don't overmix!). Blend in the melted butter. Fold in 2 cups of the toasted coconut and reserve the rest for decorating the cake. Wash the mixer beaters well and dry.

3. In another large bowl, beat the egg whites and cream of tartar with the mixer on high until frothy. Gradually add the remaining sugar and continue beating until stiff peaks form (the whites will stand up and look glossy but not dry). Using a rubber spatula, fold about one-third of the whites into the batter, then

fold in the remaining whites. Divide the batter evenly between the 2 prepared pans and bake on the middle oven rack until the tops look set and golden (not wet or sticky) and a pick inserted in the centers comes out with moist crumbs clinging to it, about 25 minutes. Touch the cakes gently in the center. When they spring back, they are done. Cool in the pans on wire racks for 15 minutes. Remove the cakes from the pans and let cool completely on the racks. Peel off the parchment liners.

4. While the cakes are baking, make the buttercream, adding the coconut extract in step 2 with the vanilla. Place a damp paper towel directly on the frosting to keep it fresh and leave at room temperature.

5. Using a serrated knife, split each cake layer in half horizontally (using a sawing motion), making 4 layers. Brush away any crumbs. Place one layer, bottom side down, on a cake plate. Spread with a ½-inch-thick layer of the buttercream and sprinkle with some of the toasted coconut. Repeat with the second layer, placing it top side down, then the third layer, also placing it top side down. Add the final layer, bottom side up, and press down slightly to be sure the layers are firmly balanced. Fill in any spaces between the layers with buttercream. Brush away any crumbs from the sides and top of the layers. Place in the freezer or refrigerator until set, 1 to 2 hours. Cover the bowl of remaining buttercream and refrigerate.

6. Using an icing spatula, frost the side and top, spreading the top with frosting ½ to ¾ inch deep and leaving enough buttercream to pipe a border around the edge. Warm the icing spatula under hot running water, dry it well, then smooth out the frosting around the side, then the top. Using the tip of a knife or a cake comb, make decorative lines across the top of the cake.

7. With your hands, gently press the remaining toasted coconut against the side of the cake, stopping at the top edge. Fit a pastry bag with a large open-star tip (#172 or #2110/1M) or a large closed-star tip (#133), fill with the remaining buttercream, and pipe swirls of rosettes or shells on the top and around the outside bottom edge of the cake. Refrigerate until time to serve. Slice the cake with a sharp straight-edge slicing knife, not a serrated knife. Cover any leftover cake and refrigerate for up to 3 days or wrap and freeze for up to 2 weeks.

Whose grandma actually made the first lemon loaf remains a mystery. However, the flavor and texture of this one are exactly what we all expect in a homemade lemon loaf: buttery, moist, rich, tender—and lots of lemon zing, thanks to fresh lemon juice and grated lemon rind. It's delicious served warm, right out of the oven, or toast a slice the next day and enjoy it for breakfast.

grandma's lemon loaf

3 cups sifted cake flour

1 tablespoon baking powder

1 teaspoon salt

$\frac{1}{2}$ teaspoon baking soda

$1\frac{1}{2}$ cups (3 sticks) unsalted butter, at room temperature

$2\frac{1}{3}$ cups sugar

5 extra-large eggs, separated

1 tablespoon pure vanilla extract

2 teaspoons pure lemon extract

$1\frac{1}{3}$ cups heavy or whipping cream

3 tablespoons lightly packed grated lemon rind

3 tablespoons fresh lemon juice

A few drops of liquid yellow food coloring or a dab of yellow icing gel

$\frac{1}{4}$ teaspoon cream of tartar

MAKES TWO 1-POUND LOAVES (8½ X 4½ X 2¾ INCHES)

1. Preheat the oven to 350°F. Generously butter the bottoms and sides of two 1-pound loaf pans (8½ x 4½ x 2¾ inches), preferably nonstick. Line the bottoms only with parchment paper. Sift together the flour, baking powder, salt, and baking soda, then place the mixture back in the sifter.

2. In a large bowl with an electric mixer (using the paddle attachment if you have it) on medium, cream the butter and sugar together until light yellow and creamy. Add the egg yolks, one at a time, beating well after each one. Beat in the extracts. Sift about one-third of the flour mixture over the batter and stir in with a wooden spoon, then stir in about one-third of the cream; repeat until both have been incorporated. Stir in the lemon rind and juice and food coloring. Wash the mixer beaters well and dry.

3. In a large bowl with the mixer on high, beat the egg whites and cream of tartar together until stiff but not dry peaks form. Using a rubber spatula, fold about one-third of the whites into the cake batter until they disappear, then gently fold in the remaining whites. Don't worry if you still see a few white specks, as they'll disappear during baking. Divide the batter equally between the 2 prepared loaf pans.

(continued on page 70)

grandma's lemon loaf (continued)

4. Bake until set and a pick inserted in the centers comes out with moist crumbs, about 45 minutes. Turn off the oven and let the loaves stay inside for 10 minutes to firm up the centers. Remove from the oven to a wire rack and let the loaves cool in the pans for 15 minutes, then remove from the pans. Peel off the parchment liners. These loaves are great warm or cold. They also freeze well, for up to 2 weeks, if you have any left!

The Junior's Way

• To ensure the centers of the loaves are perfectly baked, turn off the oven and leave them inside for 10 minutes before removing them to a rack to cool.

• Junior's serves this lemon loaf by the slice—sometimes toasted and other times à la mode. But if you would like a delicious lemony glaze, here it is (there's enough for both loaves): Heat about 1/3 cup heavy cream in a small saucepan over low heat just until lukewarm. In a bowl, stir together 2 cups sifted confectioners' sugar, 1 teaspoon grated lemon rind, 1 tablespoon fresh lemon juice, and 1 teaspoon pure lemon extract. Add only enough heavy cream until the glaze is thin enough to spread and drizzle (about 3 to 4 tablespoons). Spread on top of the cooled lemon loaves, allowing some to drizzle down the sides.

Every day is a celebration at Junior's. There always seems to be something to celebrate—a birthday, an anniversary, the last day of school, or just sharing a meal with friends. These cupcakes are perfect for any celebration, including the holidays. The bakers at Junior's start at least a month ahead to frost and decorate cupcakes in the colors of whichever holiday might be coming next— Valentine's Day, St. Patrick's Day, you name it. Feel free to decorate these cupcakes any way you want to. We suggest using buttercream in the recipe below, tinting it in whichever colors you wish, and decorating them with sprinkles and colored sugars. However, you can use any of the frostings in our Baker's Basics chapter—you can even top them with a rosette of whipped cream. Let your creativity run wild!

celebration cupcakes

FOR THE CUPCAKES
3¼ cups sifted cake flour

2 teaspoons baking powder

1 teaspoon salt

1½ cups (3 sticks) unsalted butter, at room temperature

2 cups sugar

4 extra-large eggs

1 tablespoon pure vanilla extract

1 cup whole milk (not low fat or nonfat)

FOR THE FROSTING AND DECORATION
12 cups Decorator's Buttercream (pages 132–134), tinted with food coloring (preferably icing gels) to match the holiday

Decorating sprinkles (optional)

MAKES 20 TO 22 CUPCAKES

1. Preheat the oven to 350°F. Line 22 standard muffin cups (2¾ inches in diameter) with paper, foil, or parchment liners. If you wish, pick up special holiday cupcake liners at a party or decorating shop or order them online. Sift the flour, baking powder, and salt together in a medium bowl.

2. In a large bowl with an electric mixer on medium, cream the butter and sugar together until light yellow and creamy. Add the eggs, one at a time, beating well after each one. Beat in the vanilla. Using a wooden spoon, stir in some of the flour mixture, then some of the milk. Repeat until both have been incorporated.

3. Fill the muffin cups almost to the tops of the liners (about seven-eighths full). Bake until set and a pick inserted in the centers comes out with moist crumbs, about 25 minutes. Cool in the tins for 15 minutes, then lift each cupcake out of the muffin tin with a small spatula and onto a wire rack to cool completely before frosting.

(continued on page 73)

The Junior's Way

- Chocolate ganache is another great way to frost these cupcakes. Make 3 cups ganache (pages 128-129) and place in the freezer to thicken. Then dip the tops of the cupcakes into the ganache one at a time, swirling them slightly to cover completely, then set on a wire rack. After the ganache has set, you can pipe buttercream or whipped cream swirls on top if you like!

- This recipe is the basis of Junior's all-time most popular cupcakes—their Rainbow Cupcakes. To make them, follow this recipe as directed, frosting them with a white buttercream. Cover the 1-inch decorative border with lots of rainbow sprinkles.

4. Make the buttercream. Divide it into bowls if you want a few different colors of cupcakes: red and pink for Valentine's, pink and purple for Easter, two shades of green for St. Patrick's, red and blue for the Fourth of July, black and orange for Halloween. Place a damp paper towel directly on the frosting in each bowl to keep it fresh while you work and let stand at room temperature while you work.

5. Fit a pastry bag with a medium open-star tip (such as #1M or #822) or a medium closed-star tip (such as #35 or #844). Fill the bag three-fourths full with the frosting and twist tightly to close. Starting at the outside edge, pipe the frosting continuously on top of each of the cupcakes, around and around, piping higher and higher until you reach the center. If you are using sprinkles around the edge of the cupcakes, pipe a little extra frosting all around the outside edge. With your thumbs, push the edge of the frosting down over the edge of the cupcake, slightly over the top of the liner. Using your hands, press enough sprinkles around the edge to make a 1-inch decorative border that hangs slightly over the side of the cupcake. These cupcakes are best when frosted, decorated, and served the same day. If you have a few left, store them in the refrigerator and serve the next day. Do not freeze.

Just about everyone loves peanut butter and Reese's® Peanut Butter Cups. And of course everyone loves Junior's…especially for creating this cupcake! The cake is rich and chocolaty—it's their famous devil's food recipe that they've been baking since they opened in 1950. The buttercream frosting has a whole cup of peanut butter swirled into it. The finishing touch? Peanut butter chips and a peanut butter cup, cut into pieces, perched on top.

reese's peanut butter cupcakes

MAKES 22 TO 24 CUPCAKES

FOR THE CUPCAKES

2¾ cups sifted all-purpose flour

1 tablespoon baking powder

1 teaspoon salt

½ teaspoon baking soda

1 cup (2 sticks) unsalted butter, at room temperature

1⅓ cups granulated sugar

⅓ cup firmly packed light brown sugar

3 extra-large eggs

6 ounces bittersweet chocolate (at least 60% cacao), melted and cooled

1 tablespoon unsulfured molasses (mild-flavored, not robust or blackstrap)

1 tablespoon pure vanilla extract

¾ cup whole milk (not low fat or nonfat)

1. Preheat the oven to 350°F. Line 24 standard muffin cups (2¾ inches in diameter) with paper, foil, or parchment liners. Sift the flour, baking powder, salt, and baking soda together in a medium bowl.

2. In a large bowl with an electric mixer on medium, cream the butter and both sugars together until light and creamy. Add the eggs, one at a time, beating well after each one. Beat in the melted chocolate, molasses, and vanilla. Using a wooden spoon, stir in some of the flour mixture, then some of the milk. Repeat until both have been incorporated.

3. Fill the muffin cups almost to the tops of the liners (about seven-eighths full). Bake until set and a pick inserted in the centers comes out with moist crumbs, about 25 minutes. Let cool in the tins for 15 minutes, then lift each cupcake out of the muffin tin with a small spatula and set on a wire rack to cool completely before frosting.

4. Make the buttercream, creaming the peanut butter with the butter in step 2. Place a damp paper towel directly on the frosting to keep it fresh and let stand at room temperature while you work. Cut the peanut butter cups into 6 pieces each.

FOR THE FROSTING AND DECORATION

12 cups Decorator's Buttercream (pages 132–134), adding 1 cup creamy peanut butter in step 2 when creaming the butter and shortening

24 snack-size Reese's Peanut Butter Cups, unwrapped and liners removed

Two 10-ounce packages Reese's Peanut Butter Chips

5. Fit a pastry bag with a medium open-star tip (such as #1M or #822). Fill the bag three-fourths full with the buttercream and twist tightly to close. Starting at the outside edge, pipe the frosting continuously on top of each of the cupcakes, around and around, piping higher and higher, until you reach the center. Pile 6 peanut butter cup pieces near the center of each cupcake, then almost cover the top with peanut butter chips, leaving a little of the white frosting peeking through (you will need about 3 tablespoons of chips per cupcake). These cupcakes are best when frosted, decorated, and served the same day. If you have a few left, store them in the refrigerator and serve the next day. Do not freeze.

The Junior's Way

• This cupcake uses all-purpose flour instead of cake flour for a more substantial cupcake that holds up under the buttercream frosting and all the candy decoration.

• When decorating these cupcakes, keep the edge clear so the chocolate shows through.

• We've called for two 10-ounce bags of chips so you have enough to almost entirely cover the frosting on the cupcakes not covered by the candy pieces in the center.

Junior's Pie Shoppe

"We don't tell people how they are getting their pie, we ask them how they want it! Plain, warmed up, with whipped cream, à la mode…whatever way they like. And that's how we serve it. Because pleasing our customers is what we do at Junior's," proudly exclaims Alan Rosen. And what pies they are! Fresh Strawberry Cheesecake Pie is number one on many customers' "must-have" list, filled with the same cheesecake filling that has made Junior's famous and topped with the best fresh berries they can buy. Then there are the whipped cream pies that Grandpa Harry Rosen was making even before there was a Junior's, and the apple pies they bake daily. There are pies that appear only "in season," such as their fresh peach pies, and others that show up year after year around the holidays, like their yummy sweet potato pie. No wonder folks have been stopping by Junior's for a slice of homemade pie ever since they opened their doors on Election Day in 1950.

banana whipped cream pie

MAKES ONE 9-INCH DEEP-DISH PIE, 5 TO 6 INCHES HIGH

FOR THE CRUST

1 recipe Buttery Flaky Pastry for 1 single-crust 9-inch deep-dish pie (pages 125–126)

FOR THE BANANA CUSTARD

²/₃ cup sugar

¼ cup cornstarch

3 tablespoons all-purpose flour

¼ teaspoon salt

2 cups heavy or whipping cream

1¼ cups whole milk (not low fat or nonfat)

6 extra-large egg yolks

2 tablespoons unsalted butter

1 tablespoon pure vanilla extract

1 teaspoon pure banana extract

1 to 2 drops liquid yellow food coloring (optional)

FOR THE BANANAS

2 cups sugar

1 cup water

8 large ripe bananas

FOR THE TOPPING

8 cups Decorator's Never-Fail Whipped Cream (pages 130–131)

_1._ Prepare and chill the pastry. Preheat the oven to 425°F, roll out the pastry, cut out a 15-inch circle, and fit it into a 9-inch deep-dish pie plate, leaving a 1½-inch overhang. Fold the edge of the pastry toward the outside, making a 1-inch stand-up edge, and flute. Completely blind-bake the pastry as directed for 15 minutes. Remove the pie weights (or beans/rice and parchment), cover the fluted edge of the crust with aluminum foil, and return to the oven until the bottom of the crust is dry and set, about 5 minutes. Cool completely on a wire rack.

_2._ Make the banana custard. Mix the sugar, cornstarch, flour, and salt together in a small bowl. Bring the cream and milk to a simmer in a heavy, medium saucepan over medium-high heat, just until bubbles form around the edge. Remove from the heat.

_3._ Meanwhile, in a heatproof medium bowl with an electric mixer (using the wire whip attachment if you have it), beat the egg yolks on high for 1 minute. Add the sugar mixture and beat on high until the mixture thickens and turns light yellow, about 3 minutes. On low, blend in about 1 cup of the hot cream mixture. Stir this into the hot mixture in the saucepan. Cook over medium heat, stirring constantly, until the custard thickens. Watch carefully and don't let the custard get too hot or stick to the pan. Remove from the heat and whisk in the butter and both extracts. Add a few drops of yellow food coloring if you wish. Pour into a heatproof bowl, lay a piece of plastic wrap directly on the surface of the custard (this will keep a skin from forming), and refrigerate until thickened but not set, about 1 hour.

4. While the custard is chilling, prepare the bananas. In a medium skillet, bring the sugar and water to a full rolling boil and continue to boil until it has a syruplike consistency, about 5 minutes. Remove from the heat. Peel one of the bananas and cut it into rounds about ½ inch thick. Using a slotted spoon, dip the slices into the syrup, then set on paper towels to drain (dipping the slices in the syrup will keep them from browning). Repeat with 2 or 3 more bananas until you get about 30 slices. Now, peel and halve 4 bananas vertically from one end to the other, making 8 long banana halves. Carefully dip them into the syrup and drain on a wire rack with a piece of waxed paper underneath to catch the drips.

5. To assemble the pie, make the whipped cream. Fold 1 cup of the cream into the custard, then spoon the custard into the cooled pie shell, spreading it out evenly. Cover with a ¼- to ⅜-inch layer of whipped cream. Arrange the banana rounds on top of the cream (reserve 3 to 5 for decoration). Chill the pie until completely set, about 2 hours; also refrigerate the remaining whipped cream and bananas.

6. Fit a pastry bag with a large open-star tip (such as #825 or #827) and fill three-fourths full with the remaining whipped cream. Starting at the edge of the pie, pipe the cream in sweeping swirls toward the center, going around and around, and higher and higher, until all the banana slices and the top of the pie are completely covered. The pie will resemble a small white mountain. Decorate with the 8 banana halves, rounded sides out, by arranging them vertically at equal intervals from the top of the pie down to the edge of the pie crust. Push them gently (just a little!) into the whipped cream to secure them. Pipe a large rosette of cream in the center. Stand up the 3 reserved banana slices on top. Refrigerate for at least 2 hours before serving. This pie is best served the day it is made. Refrigerate any leftover pie and serve the next day. Do not freeze.

Every day, any day, there are fresh lemon meringue pies in the Junior's bakery. You can spot them right away. They are the ones with the "mile-high" meringues and are immediately visible when you walk inside. The filling is exactly what you would expect: a custardy pudding with lots of fresh lemon flavor and lemon rind—not too stiff, not too soft, but just right to slice up perfectly every time. These tarts are equally gorgeous baked up as individual tartlets, as we do here, so each guest gets a whole little pie!

lemon meringue tartlets

MAKES 8 TARTLETS, 4½ TO 5 INCHES WIDE, 2½ TO 3 INCHES HIGH

FOR THE TARTLET SHELLS

1 recipe Buttery Flaky Pastry for tartlet shells (pages 125-126)

FOR THE LEMON CUSTARD FILLING

2 cups sugar

½ cup cornstarch

½ teaspoon salt

1¾ cups cold water

4 extra-large egg yolks

⅓ cup fresh lemon juice

3 tablespoons unsalted butter

1 tablespoon grated lemon rind

1 teaspoon pure vanilla extract

½ teaspoon pure lemon extract

FOR THE MERINGUE

4 extra-large egg whites

¼ teaspoon cream of tartar

¾ cup sugar

1. Prepare and chill the pastry. Preheat the oven to 400°F, roll out the pastry, and fit it into eight 4½- to 5-inch tartlet molds. Prick each shell and trim the edge (see The Junior's Way, page 82). Completely blind-bake the shells as directed. Cool completely on a wire rack. Leave the oven on.

2. Meanwhile, make the lemon curd filling. Mix the sugar, cornstarch, and salt together in a large, heavy saucepan. Gradually pour in the cold water, whisking continuously (important: no lumps of cornstarch should be visible). Cook, stirring constantly, over medium heat just until the mixture thickens (do not overcook or the gel could break). Remove from the heat.

3. In a medium bowl with an electric mixer (using the wire whip attachment if you have it) on high, beat the egg yolks until thickened and light yellow, about 5 minutes. Pour a little of the hot cornstarch mixture into the beaten yolks, then pour all of this egg mixture into the cornstarch mixture in the saucepan. Whisk over low heat just until the custard is hot and bubbles start to form around the edge of the pan (watch carefully, as too much heat at this stage can overcook the eggs and "separate" the custard). Remove from the heat and whisk in the lemon juice, butter, lemon rind, and both extracts. Pour the filling into the cooled tartlet shells up to the rim (you will need about ⅓ cup of filling per tartlet). Wash the mixer beaters well and dry.

4. Make the meringue. In a medium bowl with the mixer on high, beat the egg whites and cream of tartar until frothy. Gradually add the sugar, beating until stiff but not dry peaks form, about 10 minutes in all. Gently spoon the

(continued on page 82)

lemon meringue tartlets (continued)

meringue on top of each tartlet, mounding it as high as you can in the center (at least 2½ inches, preferably higher!). Seal the meringue tightly around the edge of the pastry with your finger *(very important!)*. This sealing prevents the meringue from shrinking, breaking, and weeping as it bakes and cools. With the tip of a boning or paring knife, make 6 to 8 tall peaks in each meringue.

5. Place the tartlets on a baking sheet and bake until the meringue on each is golden, about 10 minutes. Transfer the tartlets to a wire rack and cool for about 30 minutes before serving; if not serving right away, refrigerate and serve cold. These are best served the day they are made. Refrigerate any leftover tartlets and serve the next day. Do not freeze.

The Junior's Way

• If you need tartlet pans, look for ones that measure 4½ to 5 inches wide with a fluted rim, about ¾ to 1 inch high. Pans made from heavy-gauge metal are preferable because they conduct heat easily and bake and brown evenly—choose French ones made of shiny tinned steel or ones made of carbon steel with a nonstick finish. If you can find tartlet pans with removable bottoms, buy them, as their bottoms help support the baked tartlet shells while you're removing the rims and transferring the tartlets onto dessert plates.

• Here's a tip to minimize the shrinkage of these tartlet shells as they bake. First, shape each shell, making sure you do not stretch the pastry as you fit it into the tartlet mold. Prick each shell well with a fork on the bottom and especially all around the side. A small cocktail fork works well. Run your rolling pin across the top of the mold, evening off the pastry edge. Work around the inside edge of each tartlet again with your thumbs, pushing the dough gently along the bottom and up the side, ¼ to ⅜ inch above the rim. Prick the shell again. Now, if any shrinkage occurs during baking, the shells will still be at least as high as the rim of the molds.

It's no surprise—Junior's overstuffs their cherry pies with cherries! Since fresh cherries are available for only about three weeks in early summer, they use the fresh-frozen ones year-round for their pies. Use only tart red cherries for baking this pie—not the dark Bing cherries. If you cannot find either fresh or frozen red cherries, jarred or canned ones are fine; be sure to drain them well.

cherry lattice pie

FOR THE CRUST

1 recipe Buttery Flaky Pastry for one 9-inch deep-dish pie with lattice top (pages 125–126)

1 tablespoon heavy or whipping cream

FOR THE CHERRY FILLING

1¼ cups granulated sugar

⅓ cup firmly packed light brown sugar

⅓ cup quick-cooking tapioca

½ teaspoon ground nutmeg

½ teaspoon salt

2¼ pounds fresh sour red cherries, pitted (or substitute 6 cups thawed quick-frozen cherries or drained jarred or canned cherries)

2 tablespoons fresh lemon juice

1 teaspoon pure almond extract

Few drops of liquid red food coloring (optional)

3 tablespoons unsalted butter, cut into pieces

FOR BRUSHING TOP CRUST

2 tablespoons heavy or whipping cream

2 tablespoons granulated sugar

MAKES 1 OVERSTUFFED DEEP-DISH 9-INCH PIE WITH A LATTICE TOP

1. Prepare and chill the pastry. Preheat the oven to 425°F. Butter a 9-inch deep-dish pie plate.

2. In a small bowl, stir together both sugars, the tapioca, nutmeg, and salt.

3. Place the drained cherries in a large bowl. Toss with the sugar mixture until coated. Stir in the lemon juice, almond extract, and food coloring if using.

4. Remove one pastry disk from the refrigerator. Roll it out ⅛ inch thick on a lightly floured work surface and trim to a 17-inch circle. Transfer to the buttered pie plate, leaving a 2-inch overhang, and brush the inside with the cream. Spoon the cherry filling into the shell. Dot with the butter.

5. Roll out the other pastry disk ¼ inch thick. Using a fluted pastry wheel, cut out a 15-inch circle, then cut it into 10 strips, 1 inch wide. Arrange a lattice crust (see The Junior's Way, page 126) over the top of the cherries. Fold the edge of the pastry toward the outside, sealing the ends of the lattice strips and the edge of the bottom crust together. Make a 1-inch stand-up edge and flute. To decorate, brush with the cream and sprinkle with the granulated sugar.

6. Bake the pie for 15 minutes. Reduce the oven temperature to 375°F and bake until the crust is golden and the filling is bubbly, about 1 hour more. This crust is extra rich in butter, so check it occasionally during baking. When it is as brown as you like, lay aluminum foil loosely over the top of the pie for the rest of the baking time. Cool the pie on a wire rack for 5 to 6 hours before serving. It is best served the day it is made. Refrigerate any leftover pie and serve the next day. Do not freeze.

Attention all Junior's cheesecake lovers: Now you can have your favorite cheesecake in a pie! It has the same smooth cream cheese filling, topped with hand-picked ripe strawberries, a sparkling strawberry glaze, and a delicious macaroon crunch of toasted nuts and coconut.

junior's fresh strawberry cream cheese pie

MAKES ONE 9-INCH DEEP-DISH PIE

FOR THE CRUST

1 recipe Vanilla Wafer Crumb Crust (page 124), adding 1 teaspoon baking powder along with the sugar in step 1

FOR THE CREAM CHEESE FILLING

Four 8-ounce packages Philadelphia cream cheese (use only full fat), at room temperature

1 ⅔ cups sugar

¼ cup cornstarch

1 tablespoon pure vanilla extract

2 extra-large eggs

¾ cup heavy or whipping cream

FOR THE TOPPING

1 recipe Macaroon Crunch (page 139)

1 ½ to 2 quarts ripe strawberries, hulled

½ cup strawberry jelly, melted and kept warm

1. Preheat the oven to 350°F. Butter a 9-inch deep-dish pie plate. Make the crust, adding 1 teaspoon baking powder in step 1. Press the mixture over the bottom and all the way up the side of the pie plate. Freeze for 15 minutes. Bake just until set, about 10 minutes. Cool on a wire rack. Leave the oven on.

2. Make the cream cheese filling. In a large bowl with an electric mixer (using the paddle attachment if you have it) on low, beat one package of the cream cheese, ⅓ cup of the sugar, and the cornstarch together for about 3 minutes. Blend in the remaining cream cheese, one package at a time, scraping down the bowl after each one. This will take about another 3 minutes.

3. Increase the mixer speed to medium (no faster!) and beat in the remaining 1⅓ cups sugar, then the vanilla. Blend in the eggs, one at a time, beating well after each one. Beat in the cream just until completely blended. The batter will look light, creamy, and airy. *Be careful not to overmix!* Spoon the filling into the cooled crust. Bake the pie until puffed, 30 to 35 minutes. The filling will rise in the oven, then settle as it cools. Let the pie cool on a wire rack for 1 hour.

4. Meanwhile, make the Macaroon Crunch and cool.

5. Arrange the whole berries, on their sides with pointed ends out, in concentric circles on top of the pie, leaving a ½-inch border around the edge. Spoon the melted jelly over the berries, covering the top of the pie. Place the Macaroon Crunch around the edge of the pie, forming a 1- to 1½-inch border. Immediately refrigerate for at least 2 hours. The pie is best served the same day.

Since way back in the 1930s, when Grandpa Harry opened his first Enduro Sandwich Shop, then later Junior's, home-baked pies have always been part of the menu. Which fruit pies are being offered any given day depends what customers want the most and which fruits are available in the market. But whatever the season, you can always find apple pie on the menu. Here we've taken Junior's traditional apple pie and topped it off with a delicious buttery crumb topping.

apple crumb pie

MAKES 1 OVERSTUFFED 9-INCH PIE

FOR THE CRUST

1 recipe Buttery Flaky Pastry for one 9-inch single-crust deep-dish pie (pages 125–126)

FOR THE APPLE FILLING

1 cup granulated sugar

1 cup firmly packed light brown sugar

⅓ cup all-purpose flour

2 tablespoons quick-cooking tapioca

2 teaspoons ground cinnamon

¼ teaspoon ground nutmeg

½ teaspoon salt

1 teaspoon grated lemon rind

3½ pounds tart-sweet apples (see The Junior's Way, opposite)

3 tablespoons fresh lemon juice

2 tablespoons unsalted butter, cut into small pieces

1. Prepare and chill the pastry. Preheat the oven to 425°F. Butter a 9-inch deep-dish pie plate. Roll out the pastry, cut out a 15-inch circle, and fit it into the pie plate, leaving a 1½-inch overhang. Fold the edge of the pastry toward the outside, making a 1-inch stand-up edge, and flute. Place in the freezer.

2. Make the apple filling. Mix both sugars, the flour, tapioca, cinnamon, nutmeg, salt, and lemon rind together in a medium bowl.

3. Peel and core the apples. Chop enough of the apples into ½-inch dice to equal 1 cup and place in a large bowl. Slice the remaining apples into ¼-inch-thick wedges and add to the bowl (you need a total of about 10 cups of apples). Drizzle the apples with the lemon juice and stir to mix. Sprinkle the sugar mixture over the apples and toss until the slices are well coated.

4. Remove the pie shell from the freezer and spoon in the apple filling, mounding it very high in the center. Dot with the butter.

5. Make the crumb topping. Place the butter, both sugars, and the flour in a food processor in that order. Pulse about 15 seconds, just until crumbs form (do not overprocess!). Sprinkle the mixture over the top of the pie, covering it completely.

FOR THE CRUMB TOPPING

½ cup (1 stick) cold unsalted butter (not margarine), cut into pieces

½ cup firmly packed light brown sugar

½ cup granulated sugar

1 cup all-purpose flour

6. Place the pie on a baking sheet and bake for 15 minutes. Reduce the oven temperature to 375°F and bake until the crust is golden, the apples are tender, and the filling is bubbly, about 1 hour more. Test an apple slice; if it is not as tender as you like it, bake 5 to 10 minutes more. If the edge of the crust or the crumb topping browns before the pie is done, lay a piece of aluminum foil loosely over the top of the pie for the rest of the baking time.

7. Cool the pie on a wire rack for 5 to 6 hours before serving. This pie is best served the day it is made. Refrigerate any leftover pie and serve the next day. Do not freeze.

The Junior's Way

You want to use an apple variety that is firm, crisp, and won't lose its shape during baking. You also want an apple that is tart-tasting, with just a hint of sweetness. After baking many apple pies, we have found that using a combination of varieties yields the best-tasting pie—a mix of red- and green-skinned apples is a good choice. The red varieties we liked best are Braeburn, Cortland, Pink Lady, and Rome Beauty. Our green picks are Pippin, Granny Smith, Golden Delicious, and Gravenstein.

"This book has to have a Boston Cream Pie," stated Alan Rosen. And what a spectacular one this is. It's a heavenly sponge cake filled with a rich pastry cream filling and topped with deep chocolate ganache. In the mid-nineteenth century, cakes were often baked in pie pans since most homes did not have cake pans. This traditional dessert closely resembles the chocolate pudding pie, which the Parker House in Boston made famous. Hence the name Boston Cream Pie, even though it's not a pie at all!

boston cream pie

MAKES ONE 9-INCH 2-LAYER CAKE

FOR THE SPONGE CAKE

1 cup sifted cake flour

2 teaspoons baking powder

½ teaspoon salt

7 extra-large eggs, separated

1 cup sugar

1 tablespoon pure vanilla extract

½ teaspoon pure lemon extract

6 tablespoons (¾ stick) unsalted butter, melted

¼ teaspoon cream of tartar

FOR THE PASTRY CREAM

1¼ cups whole milk (not low fat or nonfat)

1 cup heavy or whipping cream

2 tablespoons unsalted butter (don't use margarine)

6 extra-large egg yolks

½ cup sugar

¼ cup cornstarch

1 tablespoon pure vanilla extract

1 to 2 drops liquid yellow food coloring (optional)

(continued on page 90)

1. Preheat the oven to 350°F. Generously butter the bottom and side of a 9-inch springform pan (preferably nonstick). Line the bottom with parchment paper (do not let the paper to come up the side). In a small bowl, sift the flour, baking powder, and salt together, then place the mixture back in the sifter.

2. In a large bowl with an electric mixer on high (use the wire whisk attachment if you have it) on high, beat the egg yolks until light yellow and slightly thickened, about 3 minutes. With the mixer running, slowly add ½ cup of the sugar and beat until thick, light yellow ribbons form, about 5 minutes. Beat in the extracts. Sift the flour mixture over the batter and stir in with a wooden spoon just until the white flecks disappear (don't overmix at this stage!). Blend in the melted butter. Wash the mixer beaters well and dry.

3. In a medium bowl with the mixer on high, beat the egg whites and cream of tartar until frothy. Gradually add the remaining ½ cup sugar and beat until stiff but not dry peaks form. Fold about one-third of the whites into the batter, then the remaining whites. Don't worry if you still see a few white specks, as they'll disappear during baking. Gently spoon the batter into the prepared springform pan.

4. Bake the cake just until set and golden (not wet or sticky), about 30 minutes. Touch the cake gently in the center. When it springs back, it is done. Watch carefully and don't let the top brown. Let cool in the pan on a wire rack for

(continued on page 90)

FOR THE GANACHE AND DECORATION

1½ cups Chocolate Ganache (pages 128–129)

4 cups Decorator's Never-Fail Whipped Cream (pages 130–131; optional)

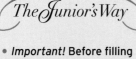

The Junior's Way

• *Important!* Before filling the cake, be sure it has cooled completely and the pastry cream is very cold and set.

• When applying the ganache, put it in a small pitcher and quickly pour it over the top. Be sure to pour a little extra near the edge of the cake so some drizzles down the side.

---

boston cream pie (continued)

30 minutes. Release the spring, remove the ring, and turn the cake out onto another rack. Remove the bottom of the pan and turn the cake over. Trim about ½ inch off the top of the cake to level it. Cool the cake completely. Wash the mixer beaters well and dry.

5. While the cake bakes, make the pastry cream. Heat the milk, cream, and butter together in a large, heavy saucepan over medium-high heat just until it bubbles around the edge, stirring until the butter has melted and is incorporated. Remove from the heat. In a large bowl with the mixer on high, beat the egg yolks, sugar, and cornstarch together until the mixture thickens and turns light yellow, about 3 minutes. On low, beat in about 1 cup of the hot cream mixture. Return this to the saucepan and stir constantly over medium heat until the mixture thickens and comes to a full boil (watch carefully, as this will take only a couple of minutes). Remove from the heat and stir in the vanilla and food coloring if using. Immediately transfer to a heatproof medium bowl, place a piece of plastic wrap directly on the surface of the pastry cream (this prevents a skin from forming), and refrigerate until cold and set, about 2½ hours.

6. When the cake and pastry cream are cold, it's time to assemble the dessert. Using a serrated knife, split the cake horizontally into 2 equal layers. Place one layer, bottom side down, on a cake plate. Spread the pastry cream evenly on the top. Set the second layer on it, top side up, pressing down gently with your fingers to level it. Refrigerate until set, about 1 hour.

7. Meanwhile, make the ganache. When it has thickened, frost the top of the cake, letting some of the ganache drizzle over the sides (see The Junior's Way, at left).

8. Prepare the whipped cream if using. Fit a pastry bag with a medium open-star tip (such as #1M or #822), fill it three-fourths full with whipped cream, and pipe a shell border around the top edge of the cake. Return the cake to the refrigerator until the ganache has set, at least 1 hour or until ready to serve. This cake is best served the day it is made. Refrigerate and serve any leftover cake the next day. Do not freeze!

Though you won't find this pie on the menu on Junior's, it uses the batter for the rich chocolate fudge brownies they're famous for and is frosted with their double-rich fudge frosting.

crustless brownie-pecan pie

MAKES ONE 11- TO 12-INCH DEEP-DISH PIE

FOR THE BROWNIE PIE FILLING

1 cup (2 sticks) unsalted butter

8 ounces bittersweet chocolate (at least 60% cacao)

1½ cups all-purpose flour

1 teaspoon salt

4 extra-large eggs

2 cups sugar

2 tablespoons pure vanilla extract

1 tablespoon unsulfured molasses (mild-flavored, not robust or blackstrap)

2 cups chopped pecans

FOR THE FROSTING AND TOPPING

4 cups Junior's Fudge Frosting (pages 135–136)

²/₃ cup large bittersweet chocolate baking chips (at least 60% cacao)

²/₃ cup coarsely chopped pecans

1. Preheat the oven to 325°F. Generously butter the bottom and side of an 11- to 12-inch quiche dish, 3 inches deep.

2. Melt the butter and chocolate together over low heat in a large, heavy saucepan, stirring until smooth. Remove from the heat and let cool while you make the batter. Mix the flour and salt together in a small bowl.

3. In a large bowl with an electric mixer on high, beat the eggs until light yellow and slightly thickened, about 3 minutes. With the mixer running, beat in the sugar. On low, blend in the chocolate mixture, then the vanilla and molasses. Using a wooden spoon, stir in the flour mixture just until the white specks disappear (do not overmix). Stir in the 2 cups chopped pecans. Spread the batter evenly in the prepared quiche dish.

4. Bake until the pie is set around the edge but not yet in the center, about 35 minutes. *Don't overbake!* To test, insert a pick in the pie about 1 inch from the edge. The crust should be soft, not hard, and very moist crumbs should cling to the pick. Now, insert the pick in the center of the pie. Thick brownie batter should cling to the pick, along with a few moist crumbs. Turn off the oven, leave the door closed, and let stand inside the oven 10 minutes more.

5. Let the pie cool in the pan on a wire rack for 1 hour. Frost the top of the pie with the Fudge Frosting (it will be about ½ inch thick) and scatter the chocolate chips and coarsely chopped pecans on top. Let cool another hour before serving. To serve, slice into wedges with a serrated cake knife. Refrigerate any leftover pie and serve within the next 2 days; or slice and freeze in an airtight freezer-safe container with waxed paper between the slices for up to 2 weeks.

Save Room
for Dessert

One evening, our waiter at Junior's advised, "Save room for dessert!" We
did, but it wasn't easy to choose which one to order. Junior's has so many
dessert offerings, some of which don't fall into the usual categories of cake
or pie. We've gathered them together into this one delicious mash-up!
You'll find some of Junior's cookie-box favorites: cookie cut-outs for the
holidays, brownies chock full of walnuts and frosted with rich fudge, and their
famous rugelach. You'll also find Belgian waffles and even fried cheesecakes.
Go ahead, save room for dessert tonight—and try one of these!

Holidays are BIG at Junior's! The baking often starts weeks ahead, with specially decorated cookies appearing in the bakery cases of all their bake shops and restaurants. The best part about making them at home? You can decorate them however you wish—and have lots of fun doing it.

holiday cookie cutouts

4½ cups all-purpose flour

1 tablespoon baking powder

1½ teaspoon salt

1 pound (4 sticks) unsalted butter, at room temperature

1¾ cups sugar

3 extra-large eggs

1 tablespoon pure vanilla extract

1 teaspoon pure lemon extract

An assortment of oven-safe candies, sprinkles, and colored sugars for decorating

The Junior's Way

It's worth shopping for decorating sugars in a baker's supply shop or on a cake decorator's website. Look for special sanding sugars and sprinkles that will not melt during baking—the colors of some even brighten in the oven.

MAKES 4 TO 5 DOZEN COOKIES

1. Mix the flour, baking powder, and salt in a medium bowl. In a large bowl with an electric mixer (using the paddle attachment if you have it) on high, cream the butter until light yellow and airy, about 2 minutes. With the mixer running, gradually add the sugar, then the eggs, one at a time, beating well after each one. Add both extracts and beat until the mixture looks creamy. Stir in the flour mixture until blended.

2. Portion the dough into 3 equal pieces and set each on a sheet of waxed paper (the dough will be a little sticky). Wrap separately and shape the packets into 6-inch disks. Refrigerate until thoroughly chilled, firm, no longer sticky, and easy to handle, about 2 hours or overnight. Before rolling out the dough, let it stand at room temperature until it's easy to work with, about 30 minutes.

3. When you're ready to bake the cookies, preheat the oven to 375°F and line 3 or 4 baking sheets (or as many as you have) with parchment paper, securing the paper to the pans with a dab of butter. Take one packet of dough from the refrigerator at a time. Roll out the dough ⅜ inch thick on a lightly floured work surface. Use cookie cutters to cut out the individual cookies close together and re-roll the dough scraps. If you have enough, re-roll the scraps and cut out more cookies. Arrange the cookies on the prepared baking sheets 1 inch apart. Decorate them with sprinkles or colored sugars as desired before baking.

4. Bake the cookies just until golden (not brown), 8 to 10 minutes. Watch carefully! Let the cookies cool on the baking sheets for 5 minutes, then carefully slide onto wire racks and cool completely for several hours. Gently place the cookies in an airtight container, separating the layers with waxed paper. Refrigerate if keeping for more than 3 days or freeze for up to 1 month.

These rugelach are buttery, cinnamony, and moist without being soft. A raisin-and-walnut filling is traditional but these get an over-the-top treatment with the addition of mini chocolate chips.

junior's rugelach

MAKES ABOUT 32 RUGELACH, 2 TO 2½ INCHES WIDE

FOR THE CREAM CHEESE PASTRY

2¼ cups all-purpose flour

1 teaspoon salt

¼ teaspoon ground mace

1 cup (2 sticks) unsalted butter, at room temperature

One 8-ounce package Philadelphia cream cheese (use only full fat), at room temperature

¾ cup confectioners' sugar

2 extra-large eggs

2 teaspoons pure vanilla extract

FOR THE CHOCOLATE-NUT FILLING

⅔ cup granulated sugar

2 teaspoons ground cinnamon

One 12-ounce package mini semi-sweet chocolate chips (2 cups)

2 cups very finely chopped walnuts (but not so fine that they look powdery)

⅓ cup fine crumbs (Macaroon Crunch, page 139, yellow cake crumbs, or vanilla wafer crumbs)

(continued on page 98)

1. Make the cream cheese pastry. Mix the flour, salt, and mace in a medium bowl. In a large bowl with an electric mixer (using the paddle attachment if you have it) on high, cream the butter and cream cheese until light yellow and creamy, about 3 minutes. Turn off the mixer, add the confectioners' sugar, then blend on high. Beat in the eggs, one at a time, beating well after each one. Beat in the vanilla. Using a wooden spoon, stir in the flour mixture just until the white specks disappear (do not overmix).

2. Turn the dough out onto a large sheet of waxed paper. Shape into a 7-inch disk and wrap it well. Refrigerate until thoroughly chilled and easy to roll, at least 4 hours or preferably overnight. If it gets too cold and firm to roll, let it stand at room temperature until easy to roll, about 30 minutes.

3. When ready to shape and bake the pastries, preheat the oven to 350°F. Line 2 baking sheets with parchment paper, securing the paper with a dab of butter. Mix the granulated sugar and cinnamon for the filling in a cup.

4. Roll out the pastry on a lightly floured work surface into a rectangle that measures 18 x 16 inches after trimming off any uneven edges. Sprinkle on the chocolate chips and lightly press them into the dough. Then sprinkle one ingredient at a time: the walnuts, crumbs, and cinnamon-sugar. Press down lightly after each addition.

5. Cut the rugelach lengthwise into 8 strips, each 2 inches wide. Cut each strip crosswise into 4 even pieces. You will have 32 pieces, each 4½ inches long and 2 inches wide. Before rolling each pastry, press the filling mixture down again lightly with your fingers. Starting with one of the narrow ends, roll up each rugelach jelly-roll style and place seam side down on the prepared baking

(continued on page 98)

FOR THE CINNAMON-SUGAR DUSTING

½ cup granulated sugar

1 tablespoon ground cinnamon

junior's rugelach (continued)

sheets ½ inch apart. Push in the sides of each pastry gently so it stands plump and high.

6. Bake the pastries just until light brown and set, 15 to 20 minutes. Watch carefully and do not overbake! While the pastries are baking, mix together the granulated sugar and cinnamon for the final dusting. As soon as the pastries come out of the oven, sprinkle them generously with the cinnamon-sugar. Cool on the baking sheets for 15 minutes, then transfer the rugelach to wire racks. Serve warm or at room temperature. Gently place the rugelach in an airtight container, separating the layers with waxed paper, and store at room temperature for up to 5 days or freeze for up to 1 month.

The Junior's Way

• Be sure the dough is thoroughly chilled. This is very important when working with cream cheese pastry.

• Take a tip from the bakers: Pile on the filling until you can't see the dough. Then lightly pat the filling into the dough with the palms of your hands. After cutting out the pastry strips, press the filling into the dough again, this time with your fingertips, before rolling up each one.

• Pinch the sides of each rugelach after placing them on the baking sheet so they stand up high and look overstuffed when baked.

Not all brownies are equal. And leave it to Junior's to make one richer in chocolate, more melt-in-your-mouth delicious, and topped with swirls of the creamy, smooth fudge frosting. We've added an extra surprise: a layer of mini chocolate chips that melts into the brownie as it bakes.

triple-the-fudge brownies

MAKES 24 BROWNIES, 2½ INCHES SQUARE AND 1½ INCHES HIGH

FOR THE BROWNIES

1 pound (4 sticks) unsalted butter

10 ounces bittersweet chocolate (at least 60% cacao)

3¼ cups all-purpose flour

2 teaspoons salt

9 extra-large eggs

4 cups sugar

2 tablespoons pure vanilla extract

4 cups coarsely chopped walnuts

One 12-ounce package mini semisweet chocolate chips (1½ cups)

(continued on page 101)

1. Preheat the oven to 325°F. Generously butter a 15½ x 10½-inch baking pan with sides 1¾ inches high or two 9-inch square baking pans with sides 2 inches high. Line the bottom and sides with parchment paper, then butter the parchment.

2. Melt the butter and chocolate over low heat in a large, heavy saucepan, stirring until smooth. Remove from the heat and let cool slightly. Mix the flour and salt together in a large bowl.

(continued on page 101)

The Junior's Way

• For fudgy, moist brownies, start with good-quality bittersweet chocolate, at least 60% cacao.

• *Important!* Bake the brownies just until they are almost set in the center—no longer.

• Here's a tip for how to get a beautiful design on the frosting: Using a small spatula (about ¾ inch wide) and starting at the top narrow left-hand corner, swirl on the diagonal, across the brownies, to the opposite right-hand bottom corner. Continue swirling on the diagonal all across the top. With a cake comb or the tip of a boning knife, make a crosshatch design, again on the diagonal, but in straight lines this time from the top narrow right-hand corner, then all across the top.

FOR THE FROSTING AND DECORATION

6 cups Junior's Fudge Frosting (pages 135-136)

24 pecan halves

3. In a large bowl with an electric mixer (using the wire whip attachment if you have it) on high, beat the eggs until light yellow and slightly thickened, about 3 minutes. With the mixer running, beat in the sugar. On low, beat in the chocolate mixture, then the vanilla. Using a wooden spoon, stir in the flour mixture just until the white specks disappear (do not overmix). Stir in the walnuts until evenly dispersed through the batter.

4. Spread half the batter in the prepared baking pan (if using two 9-inch pans, spread one-fourth in each). Sprinkle with the chocolate chips (using them all) and cover with the remaining batter. Bake just until the brownies are almost set in the center, 50 to 55 minutes for the large pan or 40 to 45 minutes for the square pans—do not overbake! The brownies are ready to come out of the oven when a pick inserted in the center comes out almost clean but still moist with some batter clinging to it.

5. Cool in the pan(s) on a wire rack for 1 hour. Turn onto the rack, peel off the parchment liners, and transfer to a large cutting board. Cool completely before frosting.

6. Make the frosting. Frost the top (it will be about ½ inch thick). Give the frosting a fancy look, if you wish (see The Junior's Way, page 99). Refrigerate until the frosting sets, about 1 hour. Slice into 2½-inch squares with a serrated knife. Top each brownie with a pecan half, rounded side up, pressing it down slightly into the frosting. Refrigerate in an airtight container, separating the layers with waxed paper, for up to 3 days or freeze for up to 1 month.

Order blintzes at Junior's and you're in for a real treat! Three golden crêpe-like pockets arrive, each stuffed with a custardy cheese filling that melts in your mouth. Blintzes are a tradition at Junior's, dating back to when Grandpa Harry Rosen first opened Junior's doors in 1950.

the best cheese blintzes

FOR THE BLINTZ WRAPPERS

2 cups all-purpose flour

⅓ cup granulated sugar

2 tablespoons cornstarch

1 teaspoon salt

8 extra-large eggs

1⅓ cups whole milk (not low fat or nonfat)

⅔ cup water

6 tablespoons (¾ stick) unsalted butter, melted, plus more butter for cooking the wrappers and frying the blintzes

Vegetable oil for cooking the wrappers

(continued on page 104)

MAKES 20 TO 24 OVERSTUFFED BLINTZES (RECIPE CAN BE DOUBLED)

1. Make the blintz wrappers. Mix the flour, granulated sugar, cornstarch, and salt together in a small bowl; set aside.

2. In a medium bowl with an electric mixer (using the wire whip attachment if you have it) on high, beat the eggs until light yellow and slightly thickened. Beat in the milk, water, and the melted butter. Reduce the speed to low and blend in the flour mixture, all at once, just until the white specks disappear. (Do not overbeat, or the blintzes could be tough.)

3. Preheat an 8- to 9-inch crêpe pan (preferably nonstick) over medium heat until a droplet of water sprinkled on the bottom dances. (Be careful not to overheat or the butter might burn.) Add a small dab of butter (about ½ teaspoon), plus a few droplets of oil (this helps keep the butter from burning). Be sure the skillet is coated well.

4. For each blintz, spoon about ¼ cup of the batter into the pan (the amount of batter you need for each blintz depends on the size of your pan). Immediately tilt the pan so the batter coats the bottom very lightly, but completely. Swirl it around and quickly pour any excess batter back into the bowl. Cook for about 30 seconds, until the bottom of the wrapper is light golden brown (lift up the edge with a butter knife to see). Loosen the wrapper by shaking the pan, then gently turn the wrapper over with a spatula (be careful not to tear it). If you're adventuresome, you might even try flipping one over by tossing it slightly in the air and catching it back in the pan. Cook the wrapper on the other side for only about 15 seconds, just until it's set. Turn it upside down onto a wire rack, so the lighter underside is up. Repeat with the remaining batter, making sure to add a little oil and butter to the pan before cooking each

(continued on page 104)

the best cheese blintzes (continued)

FOR THE CHEESE FILLING

Four 8-ounce packages
Philadelphia cream cheese (use
only full fat), at room temperature

2 cups large-curd cottage cheese

1 1/3 cups granulated sugar

2 tablespoons pure vanilla extract

FOR THE GO-ALONGS (OPTIONAL)

Fresh strawberries, hulled and
sliced vertically

Junior's Fresh Strawberry Sauce
(page 140)

Sour cream

Confectioners' sugar

wrapper. The wrappers can be refrigerated for up to 2 days or frozen for up to 1 month. To store, stack them, separating each one with plastic wrap or waxed paper. Place in a zip-top plastic bag.

5. Make the cheese filling. In a medium bowl with an electric mixer on medium, beat the cream cheese, cottage cheese, granulated sugar, and vanilla together just until thoroughly mixed.

6. Assemble the blintzes. Working with one wrapper at a time, spoon about 1/4 cup filling in the center on the lightly cooked side (not the golden brown side) of each wrapper, then fold the edges over like an envelope (see The Junior's Way, below). Preheat the oven to 275°F.

7. Fry the blintzes. Melt 2 to 3 tablespoons butter (just butter this time, no oil) in a large skillet over medium heat. Place one-third to one-half of the filled blintzes (depending upon the size of your skillet), folded side down, in the skillet. Fry, turning once, until golden on both sides and hot all the way through (*important!*), about 5 minutes total. Transfer to a baking sheet and keep hot in the oven. Repeat with the rest of the blintzes.

8. Serve the blintzes hot, garnished with a few slices of strawberries and accompanied by small bowls of the strawberry sauce and sour cream, if you like. Spoon some confectioners' sugar into a tea strainer and apply a fine sprinkling over the blintzes and the plate. Serve immediately; do not store blintzes once they have been filled and fried.

The Junior's Way

• Cook a "test" crêpe first, to check that your pan is buttered correctly and the heat is not too hot.

• Pour the batter into the pan in a circular motion, making sure the bottom is covered. Then swirl and tilt the pan, letting some of the bat-ter come up the sides about 1/4 to 3/8 inch. This makes it easier to pick up a little edge to check how brown the crêpe is cooking.

• Success in making blintzes is all in the folding. Spoon the filling in the center of the blintz wrapper, then fold the ends over like an envelope: first the top edge, then the left side, next the right side, and finally the bottom edge. Be sure the filling is completely enclosed. Place the blintzes, folded sides down, in the skillet. As they fry, the heat seals the edges shut.

It's time for a party—and here's an absolute "must" for the menu: Mini cheesecakes with that same heavenly, dreamy flavor and melt-in-your-mouth creaminess of Junior's larger cheesecakes. Instead of a crust, we've used the finest sprinkling of crumbs made from their signature sponge cake. Or, if you're in a hurry, you can forget those and just spoon the filling into the little liners (they bake up just fine). These disappear fast, as few folks can eat only one.

mini cheesecakes

1 recipe 9-inch Sponge-Cake Crust (page 15), baked and turned into Decorator Cake Crumbs (page 127); optional

Three 8-ounce packages Philadelphia cream cheese (use only full fat), at room temperature

1⅓ cups granulated sugar

3 tablespoons cornstarch

1 tablespoon pure vanilla extract

2 extra-large eggs

⅔ cup heavy or whipping cream

Confectioners' sugar (about ½ cup); optional

MAKES FORTY-EIGHT 2-BITE, 2-OUNCE MINI CHEESECAKES, ABOUT 2 INCHES IN DIAMETER AND 1 INCH HIGH

1. Preheat the oven to 350°F. Bake the sponge cake and turn it into Decorator Cake Crumbs if using. Leave the oven on.

2. In a large bowl with an electric mixer (using the paddle attachment if you have it) on low, beat together 1 package of the cream cheese, ⅓ cup of the granulated sugar, and the cornstarch for about 3 minutes to make a stable starter batter. Blend in the remaining cream cheese, 1 package at a time, scraping down the bowl after adding each one. This will take about another 3 minutes.

3. Increase the mixer speed to medium (no faster!) and beat in the remaining 1 cup granulated sugar, then the vanilla. Blend in the eggs, one at a time, beating well after each one, then the cream. The batter will look light, creamy, airy, and almost like billowy clouds. *Be careful not to overmix!*

4. Set out two 2-ounce mini muffin tins (each with 24 cups 2 inches in diameter and 1 inch deep). Line with paper, foil, or parchment liners. Sprinkle a thin layer of cake crumbs on the bottom of each cup, if using. (You will not need all the crumbs for these cheesecakes, so freeze the extra to use to top puddings or ice cream later.) Gently spoon the batter into the muffin cups, up to the tops of the liners.

5. Place one of the muffin tins in the center of a large shallow pan and pour hot water in it so it comes about 1 inch up the sides of the tin. Bake until the tops of the little cakes are puffed and just beginning to brown around the

(continued on page 106)

edges, about 20 minutes (do not overbake, as the small cakes might sink in the center as they cool). Remove the tin from the water bath and transfer to a wire rack. Set the second tin in the water bath, replenish the water if necessary, and bake. Let the cheesecakes cool on a wire rack at room temperature for 2 hours, then cover with aluminum foil and refrigerate until completely cold, preferably overnight or for at least 4 hours. If you are not serving all 48 mini cakes, wrap and freeze the extras for up to 1 month before decorating them.

6. To serve these little cakes the Junior's way, present them plain, in all of their glory, or shower the cold mini cheesecakes with a little confectioners' sugar (see The Junior's Way, below). Place the mini cakes, still in their liners, on a serving platter and refrigerate until serving time.

The Junior's Way

To sprinkle these tiny cheesecakes with confectioners' sugar, place a small amount of the sugar in a tea strainer. Holding the strainer about 2 inches above the cold cakes, tap the side of the strainer gently with your finger until the little cakes are lightly showered with the sugar.

"You really fry your cheesecake?" I asked Alan. "Sure! It's easy and delicious!" he assured me. "Our customers love it. Try it!" So I left Junior's, headed back to the test kitchen, and tried it. As usual, Alan was right. The fried cake came out golden and crispy on the outside, soft on the inside. If you like, serve it with fresh strawberries or Junior's Fresh Strawberry Sauce (page 140).

fried cheesecake

1 to 4 very cold slices Junior's Original New York Cheesecake (pages 12-15), each 3 inches wide and about 2½ inches high

4 extra-large eggs

¼ cup whole milk

1 cup corn flake crumbs

Oil with a high smoke point, such as canola oil

MAKES ENOUGH BATTER TO FRY 4 SLICES OF CHEESECAKE

1. Cut the cheesecake into pie-shaped slices with the widest area (at the back of the slice) measuring about 3 inches. Whisk the eggs and milk together until frothy. Dip the slices first in the egg batter, then roll in the crumbs until well coated. Refrigerate for 5 to 10 minutes to set.

2. Meanwhile, heat enough oil to completely cover the cheesecake slices, at least 4 to 5 inches deep, to 350° to 360°F (no hotter!) in a deep fryer, Dutch oven, or deep sauté pan. Slide a coated slice of cheesecake into the hot oil, completely immersing it. Cook each slice for 2 to 3 minutes, just until golden and crispy. Using a large slotted spatula with a long handle, transfer the cheesecake to paper towels to drain, then serve while still warm.

The Junior's Way

• Be sure to use a deep fryer or heavy pan that holds enough oil so the slice is completely immersed during frying; this ensures that the whole slice fries at the same time, at the same temperature, all at once.

• Use only fresh, clean oil that has not been used for frying other foods.

• Use a deep-fat frying thermometer and check the temperature frequently. Keep it between 350° and 360°F—no hotter.

• Be sure the slice of cheesecake is very cold before starting.

Everything seems oversized, overstuffed, and over-the-top at Junior's, even their waffles. These dessert waffles are slightly sweeter and richer than the Belgian waffles served in Junior's restaurants.

belgian waffles à la mode

MAKES TWELVE 4½-INCH SQUARE BELGIAN WAFFLES AND 4 CUPS SAUCE

FOR THE WAFFLES

1 cup all-purpose flour

1 cup cake flour

⅓ cup sugar

1 tablespoon baking powder

1 teaspoon salt

4 extra-large eggs

1½ cups heavy or whipping cream

½ cup whole milk

½ cup (1 stick) unsalted butter, melted

1 tablespoon plus 1 teaspoon pure vanilla extract

FOR THE HOT APPLE-RAISIN SAUCE

2⅓ cups apple cider

1 cup sugar

½ teaspoon ground cinnamon

⅛ teaspoon salt

2 pounds firm red apples (such as Cortland, Gala, or Rome Beauty) peeled, cored, and cut into 1-inch chunks

⅔ cup dark raisins

1½ tablespoons cornstarch

2 teaspoons pure vanilla extract

¼ teaspoon pure lemon extract

FOR SERVING

Vanilla bean ice cream

1. Make the waffle batter. In a large bowl, mix both flours, the sugar, baking powder, and salt together. Make a well in the center with a large spoon. In a medium bowl with an electric mixer on high, beat the eggs until light yellow and slightly thickened, about 3 minutes. Beat in the cream, milk, melted butter, and vanilla until well combined. Pour this mixture all at once into the well in the dry ingredients. Using a wooden spoon, stir the dry ingredients into the wet ones until well blended (don't worry if a few white specks of flour remain). Let stand at room temperature while you make the sauce.

2. Make the Hot Apple-Raisin Sauce. Combine 2 cups of the cider, the sugar, cinnamon, and salt in a large, heavy saucepan. Bring to a full boil over high heat and let boil for 5 minutes. Add the apples and raisins, reduce the heat to medium, and simmer until the apples are tender and the raisins are plump, about 15 minutes. Stir occasionally to keep the apples from sticking.

3. Mix the cornstarch and the remaining ⅓ cup cider together in a cup until the cornstarch thoroughly dissolves. Whisking constantly, drizzle this into the hot cider mixture. Bring to a full boil and continue to boil until it thickens slightly, about 2 minutes (stir constantly to avoid sticking). Immediately remove the pan from the heat. Stir in the extracts. Cover to keep warm.

4. Preheat the oven to 275°F. Preheat your waffle iron, then bake the waffles according to the manufacturer's directions. As they finish cooking, transfer the waffles to a baking sheet and keep warm in the oven.

5. To serve, place one waffle on a dessert plate, set a giant scoop of ice cream on top, and spoon a helping of the warm apple-raisin sauce over all. Freeze any leftover waffles for up to 2 weeks in zip-top plastic freezer bags.

For Those Watching Their Sugar

"We at Junior's realize there are many people on sugar-restricted diets who cannot eat sugar for medical reasons or who often skip dessert because they are watching their weight," explains Alan. "We believe they deserve great-tasting sugar-free alternatives and should be able to enjoy dessert—without the guilt." That's what this chapter is all about: a way to have your cheesecake without going off your diet. We've included sugar-free versions for some of Junior's most popular desserts, including their Original New York and Raspberry Swirl cheesecakes. And we've created all of the recipes in this chapter to contain no processed sugar but a natural sugar substitute instead. Also, check out the shopping guide on page 112; it will make your sugar-free shopping a snap. Because at Junior's, we care.

Sugar-Smart Shopping List

Whether you are following a no-sugar or low-sugar diet, you need to buy the right ingredients when baking sugar-free. If you do, you'll end up with desserts that taste just as scrumptious as those made using sugar. Reesa Sokoloff, a registered dietitian and CEO of the Sweet Life, offers the following shopping tips for the sugar-free baker.

In the Produce Section

• Buy fresh fruits or unsweetened frozen ones—not canned fruit, as it is often packed in sugar syrup.

• Reach for fruit low in fructose (natural sugar), such as berries, peaches, nectarines, pears, apples, cantaloupe, and honeydew.

• Avoid fruits very high in natural sugars, such as grapes and bananas.

In the Baking Aisle

• Whenever possible, substitute nut flour for wheat flour. Wheat flour, such as all-purpose and cake flours, is broken down into sugar in your body; this is not the case with nut flours. In the recipes in this chapter, we either call for all almond flour or a combination of almond flour and all-purpose or cake flour. Almond flour (also sometimes labeled as almond meal) is made from ground blanched almonds and can be found in some large supermarkets, health food stores, specialty food stores, and online.

• Use sugar substitutes instead of sugar. When baking, you have two primary choices, Xylitol, a natural sweetener, and granulated Splenda®, which is specially formulated for baking. Junior's uses Xylitol in all its sugar-free desserts, so it is what we've used throughout this chapter. It is a naturally occurring carbohydrate found in fibrous vegetables and fruits that tastes similar to sugar and will not break down when exposed to heat, so you can easily bake with it. In general, you need about a third less Xylitol than sugar when reformulating recipes. Look for it in health food stores, vitamin stores, specialty drugstores, or online. Be sure to choose the 100% product, without any anti-caking agents.

• The darker the better when shopping for chocolate. Choose extra bittersweet (70% cacao) or unsweetened (100% cacao), not bittersweet, semisweet, milk chocolate, or white chocolate—all of which are higher in sugar.

• Unsweetened is the way to go with cocoa and coconut. Be sure to buy dark unsweetened cocoa powder (100% cacao), not cocoa mix, which contains sugar. Avoid sweetened coconut; you may need to look for unsweetened coconut in your supermarket's freezer section or the health food store.

• Use low-carbohydrate thickeners, such as cream of tartar or arrowroot; skip the cornstarch, as it breaks down to sugar in your body.

In the Dairy Case

• Choose heavy or whipping cream, instead of light cream or half-and-half, which contain more milk sugar.

• Reach for full-fat cream cheese, instead of reduced-fat or nonfat. The reduced products will break down in the oven.

• As for eggs, use as many as you like.

• When reaching for sour cream, choose full fat, not low fat or nonfat; again, those with reduced fat contain more milk sugar.

Enjoy shopping and baking the sugar-smart way!

There really is a way to bake Junior's Original New York Cheesecake the sugar-free way. We've used the same recipe, the same preparation steps, and the same baking techniques that have made Junior's famous. We've just left out the sugar and used a shortbread crust instead of the traditional sponge-cake crust.

junior's sugar-free new york cheesecake

MAKES ONE 9-INCH CHEESECAKE, ABOUT 2 ¼ INCHES HIGH

FOR THE ALMOND SHORTBREAD CRUST

⅔ cup almond flour (opposite)

⅓ cup all-purpose flour

2 tablespoons Xylitol sweetener (opposite)

1 teaspoon salt

½ cup (1 stick) cold unsalted butter, cut into small pieces

1 extra-large egg yolk, slightly beaten with fork

1 to 2 tablespoons heavy or whipping cream

FOR THE CHEESECAKE FILLING

Four 8-ounce packages Philadelphia cream cheese (use only full fat), at room temperature

1 cup Xylitol sweetener

3 tablespoons arrowroot, dissolved in 2 tablespoons cold water

2 tablespoons pure vanilla extract

2 extra-large eggs

¾ cup heavy or whipping cream

1. Preheat the oven to 350°F. Generously butter the bottom and side of a 9-inch springform pan (preferably nonstick). Wrap the outside with aluminum foil, covering the bottom and extending all the way up the side, so water will not leak into the cake as it bakes.

2. Make the shortbread crust. Place both flours, the Xylitol, and salt in a food processor and process for 15 seconds. Add the butter and pulse until the mixture pulls together, about 30 seconds. Add the egg yolk and 1 tablespoon of the cream. Pulse until a soft, slightly sticky dough forms. If it is still stiff, add another tablespoon of cream. Flour your fingers and gently press the dough into the bottom of the prepared springform pan until it is covered. Bake the crust just until it no longer looks moist on the top and feels set when you touch it *(do not overbake!)*, 7 to 8 minutes. Cool in the pan on a wire rack. Leave the oven on.

3. Make the cheesecake filling. In a large bowl with an electric mixer (using the paddle attachment if you have it) on low, beat one package of the cream cheese, ½ cup of the Xylitol, and the dissolved arrowroot for about 3 minutes to make a stable starter batter. Blend in the remaining cream cheese, one package at a time, scraping down the bowl after adding each one. This will take about another 3 minutes.

(continued on page 114)

junior's sugar-free new york cheesecake (continued)

4. Increase the mixer speed to medium *(no faster!)* and beat in the remaining ½ cup Xylitol, then the vanilla. Add the eggs, one at a time, beating well after each one. Beat in the cream just until completely blended. The batter will look light, creamy, airy, and almost like billowy clouds. *Be careful not to overmix!*

5. Spoon the batter over the baked shortbread crust. Place the springform pan in the center of a large shallow pan and add hot water to the larger pan so that it comes about 1 inch up the side of the springform. Bake until the edge is light golden brown and the cake is light yellow-beige, about 1¼ hours. If the center is still very jiggly, let the cake bake for 5 to 10 minutes more.

6. Gently remove the cake from the water bath, transfer it to a wire rack, remove the foil, and leave it on the rack (just walk away—don't move it) for 2 hours, even 4 hours, it doesn't matter. The less you move it, the less likely it is the cake will crack. Once it has cooled, leave the cake in the pan, cover loosely with plastic wrap, and refrigerate overnight, until it is completely cold.

7. To serve, remove the springform ring from the cake and serve from the bottom of the pan (do not try to transfer it to a serving platter). Cover any leftover cake and refrigerate for up to 3 days. Do not freeze this cake.

The Junior's Way

If you do not have a food processor, when making the shortbread crust, cut the butter into the flour mixture with a pastry cutter until crumbs the size of peas form. Then mix the dough with a wooden spoon.

Here's one of Junior's favorite cheesecakes, made the sugar-free way. The cheesecake is based on their original recipe, using the natural sugar substitute Xylitol (see page 112 for more about it). The swirl is made from unsweetened raspberries, one of the fruits lowest in natural sugars. And the design is easy to create but so impressive after baking! It'll "wow" your guests!

sugar-free raspberry swirl cheesecake

MAKES ONE 9-INCH CHEESECAKE, ABOUT 2½ INCHES HIGH

FOR THE ALMOND SHORTBREAD CRUST

⅔ cup almond flour (page 112)

⅓ cup all-purpose flour

2 tablespoons Xylitol sweetener (page 112)

1 teaspoon salt

½ cup (1 stick) cold unsalted butter, cut into small pieces

1 extra-large egg yolk, slightly beaten with fork

1 to 2 tablespoons heavy or whipping cream

FOR THE RASPBERRY SWIRL

1 pound frozen unsweetened raspberries, thawed and drained

3 tablespoons Xylitol sweetener

2 tablespoons arrowroot, dissolved in 2 tablespoons cold water

(continued on page 116)

1. Preheat the oven to 350°F. Generously butter the bottom and side of a 9-inch springform pan (preferably nonstick). Wrap the outside with aluminum foil, covering the bottom and extending all the way up the side, so water will not leak into the cake as it bakes.

2. Make the shortbread crust. Place both flours, the Xylitol, and salt in a food processor and process for 15 seconds. Add the butter and pulse until the mixture pulls together, about 30 seconds. Add the egg yolk and 1 tablespoon of the cream. Pulse until a soft, slightly sticky dough forms. If it is still stiff, add another tablespoon of cream. Flour your fingers and gently press the dough into the bottom of the prepared springform pan until it is covered. Bake the crust just until it no longer looks moist on the top and feels set when you touch it *(do not overbake!)*, 7 to 8 minutes. Cool in the pan on a wire rack. Leave the oven on.

3. Make the raspberry swirl. Pulse the drained berries in a food processor until puréed, about 30 seconds. Strain the purée into a small bowl to remove the seeds. Whisk in the Xylitol and dissolved arrowroot.

(continued on page 116)

FOR THE CHEESECAKE FILLING

Four 8-ounce packages
Philadelphia cream cheese (use
only full fat), at room temperature

1 cup Xylitol sweetener

3 tablespoons arrowroot, dissolved
in 2 tablespoons cold water

2 tablespoons pure vanilla extract

2 extra-large eggs

¾ cup heavy or whipping cream

The Junior's Way

The bakers at Junior's pipe the raspberry swirls on each and every cake by hand—first on top, then inside the cake, creating beautiful swirls throughout the batter. This requires lots of skill! You can also get lovely swirls inside the cake by sandwiching some purée between two layers of white cheesecake batter, then piping the rest on top. Dragging a skewer or the tip of a boning knife through the piped design adds a professional look. Even if you're just learning to bake, you can serve a cake that you'll be proud of.

4. Make the cheesecake filling. In a large bowl with an electric mixer (using the paddle attachment if you have it) on low, beat one package of the cream cheese, ½ cup of the Xylitol, and the dissolved arrowroot for about 3 minutes to make a stable starter batter. Blend in the remaining cream cheese, one package at a time, scraping down the bowl after adding each one. This will take about another 3 minutes.

5. Increase the mixer speed to medium *(no faster!)* and beat in the remaining ½ cup Xylitol, then the vanilla. Add the eggs, one at a time, beating well after each one. Beat in the cream just until completely blended. The batter will look light, creamy, airy, and almost like billowy clouds. *Be careful not to overmix!*

6. Gently spoon half the cheesecake batter over the baked shortbread crust. Randomly spoon 4 or 5 tablespoons of the raspberry purée over the batter, a tablespoon at a time. Then spread the remaining batter in the pan, covering the purée layer. Fit a pastry bag with a small round tip (such as #2 or #3). Fill the bag with the remaining purée. Quickly turn the bag upright and make multiple swirls in a flower design on top of the cake. Take a skewer or a boning knife and drag it through the purée, in different directions, creating a marbled effect.

7. Place the springform pan in the center of a large shallow pan and add hot water to the larger pan until it comes about 1 inch up the side of the spring-form. Bake until the edge is light golden tan and the swirl is dark raspberry-colored, about 1¼ hours. If the center is still very jiggly, let the cake bake for 5 to 10 minutes more.

8. Gently remove the cake from the water bath, transfer it to a wire rack, remove the foil, and leave it on the rack (just walk away—don't move it) for 2 hours, even 4 hours, it doesn't matter. The less you move it, the less likely it is the cake will crack. Once it has cooled, leave the cake in the pan, cover loosely with plastic wrap, and refrigerate overnight, until it is completely cold.

9. To serve, remove the springform ring from the cake and serve from the bottom of the pan (do not try to transfer the cake to a serving platter). Cover any leftover cake and refrigerate for up to 3 days. Do not freeze this cake.

Attention all lemon lovers—this cake is three layers of delicious lemony flavor stacked with a heavenly lemon whipped-cream mousse.

sugar-free lemon mousse triple-layer cake

FOR THE CAKE

¾ cup sifted cake flour

⅔ cup almond flour (page 112)

1 tablespoon baking powder

½ teaspoon salt

9 extra-large eggs, separated

¾ cup plus 2 tablespoons Xylitol sweetener (page 112)

1 tablespoon pure vanilla extract

1 teaspoon pure lemon extract

½ cup (1 stick) unsalted butter, melted

¼ teaspoon cream of tartar

FOR THE LEMON MOUSSE

1½ quarts (6 cups) icy-cold heavy or whipping cream

1½ teaspoons cream of tartar

3 tablespoons Xylitol sweetener

1½ tablespoons pure vanilla extract

2 teaspoons pure lemon extract

1 tablespoon grated lemon rind

Yellow food gel or food coloring

MAKES ONE 9-INCH 3-LAYER CAKE, ABOUT 2½ INCHES HIGH

1. Preheat the oven to 350°F. Generously butter the bottom and side of a 9-inch springform pan. Line the bottom only with parchment paper (don't let the paper come up the side) and butter the parchment well. Mix both flours, the baking powder, and salt together in a medium bowl.

2. In a large bowl with an electric mixer (using the paddle attachment if you have it) on high, beat the egg yolks for 3 minutes. With the mixer running, slowly add ¾ cup of the Xylitol and beat until thick, light yellow ribbons form, about 5 minutes more. Beat in the extracts. On low, blend in the flour mixture just until the white flecks disappear. *Be careful not to overmix!* Blend in the melted butter.

3. In another large bowl with the mixer (using the whisk attachment if you have it) on high, beat the egg whites and cream of tartar until frothy. Add the remaining 2 tablespoons Xylitol and beat until stiff peaks form (the whites will stand up and look glossy but not dry). Fold about one-third of the whites into the batter, then the remaining whites. Don't worry if you still see a few white specks, as they'll disappear during baking.

4. Spoon the batter into the prepared springform pan and bake until the top looks set and golden (not wet or sticky) and a pick inserted in the center comes out with moist crumbs clinging to it, 45 to 50 minutes. Touch the cake gently in the center. When it springs back, it is done. Turn the oven off and let the cake stand in the warm oven with the door closed for 5 minutes. Transfer to a wire rack and cool in the pan for 30 minutes. Remove the ring, turn the cake onto the rack, peel off the parchment liner, and turn the cake top side up. Cool for another 30 minutes, then refrigerate until cold, 1 to 2 hours.

(continued on page 120)

sugar-free lemon mousse triple-layer cake (continued)

5. When ready to assemble and frost the cake, chill a large bowl and the mixer beaters. Cut off about ½-inch-thick layer from the top of the cake, leveling it. Use this to make Decorator Cake Crumbs (page 127). (You need about 2 cups of crumbs.)

6. Make the lemon mousse. In the chilled bowl with the mixer (using the whisk attachment if you have it) on high, whip the cream and cream of tartar just until the mixture begins to thicken. Add the Xylitol and both extracts and beat until the cream stands up in stiff peaks but is still soft enough to flow. Don't overbeat or the cream will curdle. Transfer about 3 cups of the cream to a small bowl for piping the white rosette border later. Fold the lemon rind into the remaining mousse and color it a pale yellow. Cover both bowls and refrigerate.

7. Assemble the cake. With a serrated knife, cut the cake horizontally into 3 equal layers, using a sawing motion. Each layer will be about ½ inch high. Brush away any loose crumbs. Place the first layer, bottom side down, on a serving plate that can go into the freezer. Spread it with a layer of the lemon mousse, about ¼ inch thick. Stack on the next cake layer, top side down, and spread with a ¼-inch-thick layer of mousse, then top with the last layer, top side down. Brush away any loose crumbs on the top and side. Frost the top with a ½-inch-thick layer of the mousse. Fill in any spaces around the side with extra mousse. Run the icing spatula over the top and around the side to smooth out the mousse. Place the cake preferably in the freezer, if you have the space, or in the refrigerator until the mousse has set, 2 to 3 hours. Refrigerate the remaining lemon mousse.

8. To finish, frost the side with the lemon mousse (reserve a little of it for the final decoration), covering all edges, up to the top edge of the cake. Run the spatula around the side to smooth it. Cover the side (but not the top) with the cake crumbs, pressing them into the mousse with your fingers and covering it well.

9. Fit a pastry bag with a large closed-star tip (such as #845 or #846), and fill the bag three-fourths full with the reserved whipped cream. Pipe 10 rosettes an equal distance apart on the top about 1 inch away from the edge. Color the last of the lemon mousse a bright golden yellow. Fit a clean pastry bag with a small round open tip (such as a #1 or #2) and fill with the golden mousse. Use to make the bright yellow centers of the flowers. Refrigerate the cake for at least 1 hour or until serving time (but not more than 6 hours). This cake is best the day it is made. Refrigerate any leftover cake and serve the next day. Do not freeze.

The Junior's Way

Take a tip from the bakers: When frosting a cake with a whipped-cream mousse, you want both the mousse and the cake to be as cold as possible. Place the cake and the bowl of mousse in the refrigerator until you're ready to put the two together.

Here are the same fresh apples that Junior's uses in their apples pies, this time baked up in an almond tart shell and topped with fresh raspberries. The best part? Each slice is sugar-free but still tastes great!

sugar-free apple-berry tart

MAKES ONE 11-INCH TART

FOR THE ALMOND CRUST

8 ounces slivered blanched almonds (about 2 cups)

1/3 cup almond flour (page 112)

1 1/2 tablespoons Xylitol sweetener (page 112)

1/2 teaspoon baking powder

1/2 teaspoon salt

1/2 teaspoon almond extract

1/2 cup (1 stick) unsalted butter, melted

FOR THE APPLE-RASPBERRY FILLING

1 pound tart-sweet red apples (such as Braeburn, Pink Lady, or Rome Beauty)

1 pound green apples (such as Granny Smith)

2 cups water

3 tablespoons heavy cream

2 tablespoons unsalted butter, melted

1 tablespoon Xylitol sweetener

1 teaspoon ground cinnamon

One 6-ounce carton fresh raspberries (about 1 cup), cut in half

1. Preheat the oven to 350°F. Generously butter the bottom and side of an 11-inch tart pan with 1-inch sides (preferably nonstick with a removable bottom).

2. Make the almond crust. Place the almonds in a food processor and pulse until finely chopped (not ground), about 1 minute. Add the flour, Xylitol, baking powder, salt, and almond extract and process for 15 seconds more to mix. With the processor running, add the melted butter through the feed tube and process until the mixture comes together in a dough, about 10 seconds. Press the dough over the bottom and all the way up the side of the prepared tart pan. Prick with a fork; put in the freezer 10 minutes. Bake just until set and golden (*do not overbake!*), 8 to 10 minutes. Leave the oven on.

3. Meanwhile, peel, core, and vertically cut the apples into thin slices (about 1/8 inch thick). Bring the water to a simmer over medium heat and poach the apples for 1 to 2 minutes, just until crisp-tender. Transfer to paper towels with a slotted spoon to drain. Brush the tart shell with the cream, then arrange the apples in the crust in concentric circles, overlapping the slices and each row slightly. Drizzle with the melted butter. Mix the Xylitol with the cinnamon and sprinkle over the apples.

4. Bake the tart until the apples are tender, about 25 minutes. Transfer to a wire rack. While the tart is still hot, scatter the raspberries, cut side down, on top. Cool for about 30 minutes. Remove the ring of the pan, leave the tart on the bottom, and place on a cake plate. Serve warm or at room temperature. Do not freeze.

Baker's Basics

Junior's has many "regulars" — that is, customers who have been coming to the restaurant for years, some each morning for Danish and coffee, others for Saturday night dinner or family celebrations, year after year. They know that whatever they order, it will always be great. These basic recipes are part of the reason. Here you'll find many of Junior's signature recipes: Fresh Strawberry Sauce, Junior's Cream Cheese Frosting, the chocolate ganache they use to decorate cakes, cheesecakes, and cupcakes, and many others.

According to Alan Rosen, crusts should be a platform for a pie or cake—not overpower them in texture or flavor. This crust adds just a hint of sweetness and richness to whipped cream pies, mini cheesecakes, and ice cream pies.

vanilla wafer crumb crust

50 vanilla wafers, such as Nabisco Nilla® Wafers

⅓ cup sugar

6 to 8 tablespoons (¾ to 1 stick) unsalted butter, melted

The Junior's Way

If you don't have a food processor, place about half the cookies in a gallon-size zip-top plastic bag. Leave about an inch opened to allow the air to escape. Using a rolling pin, roll back and forth several times over the bag, turning it over a few times, until the cookie crumbs are as fine as you like them. Repeat with the remaining cookies.

MAKES ONE 8- OR 9-INCH CRUMB CRUST WITH 2-INCH-HIGH SIDES

1. Pulse the wafers in a food processor about 30 seconds, until you have fine, even crumbs. Add the sugar and process a few seconds more. You will have about 2 cups of crumbs.

2. With the processor running, slowly add 6 tablespoons of the melted butter through the feed tube and process until the crumbs are moist and come together. Add a little more butter if needed. Shape the crust as the recipe directs.

CHOCOLATE WAFER CRUMB CRUST

Prepare as for Vanilla Wafer Crumb Crust, above, adding 3 tablespoons unsweetened dark cocoa powder (100% cacao) with the sugar.

OREO CHOCOLATE CRUMB CRUST

Prepare as for Vanilla Wafer Crumb Crust, above, using 30 Oreos or other chocolate sandwich cookies instead of the vanilla wafers. Pull the Oreos apart and scrape away and discard the filling before turning the cookies into crumbs as directed.

FAMOUS CHOCOLATE CRUMB CRUST

Prepare as for Vanilla Wafer Crumb Crust, above, substituting Nabisco Famous Chocolate Wafers for the vanilla wafers and adding 3 tablespoons unsweetened dark cocoa powder (100% cacao) along with the sugar. You'll need only 6 tablespoons melted butter for this crust.

As any baker knows, a great pie starts with a great crust. We've taken Junior's recipe and added a little more butter for extra richness. This one is quickly made in the food processor, but you can also make it in a stand mixer, using the paddle attachment if you have it. However you make it, this crust will always bake up golden, flaky, and crispy, pie after pie. We give you options for making a double-crust pie, a deep-dish pie with lattice, and tartlets.

buttery flaky pastry

FOR ONE 8- TO 9-INCH DEEP-DISH PIECRUST WITH LATTICE TOP

½ cup ice water

2 extra-large egg yolks, slightly beaten

1½ tablespoons fresh lemon juice

2⅔ cups all-purpose flour

1⅓ cups cake flour

¼ cup sugar

1½ teaspoons salt

1 teaspoon baking powder

1 cup (2 sticks) cold unsalted butter, cut into ½-inch cubes

6 tablespoons vegetable shortening

(continued on page 126)

1. In a small bowl, whisk the water, egg yolk, and lemon juice together; set aside. Place both flours, the sugar, salt, and baking powder in the food processor and process for a few seconds to mix. Add the butter and shortening if called for and pulse until coarse crumbs form. With the motor running, slowly pour the lemon-egg-water mixture through the feed tube, adding a little more water, 1 teaspoon at a time, if needed, until the dough holds together. Process for about 30 seconds more, just until a ball of pastry forms.

For a deep-dish piecrust with lattice top: Shape the dough into two 7-inch disks and wrap in plastic. Chill for at least 1 hour. See the Junior's Way (page 126) for how to make the lattice.

For a single deep-dish piecrust: Shape the dough into a 5-inch disk and wrap in plastic. Chill for at least 1 hour.

For tartlet shells: Shape the dough into a 5-inch disk and wrap in plastic. Chill for at least 1 hour.

2. *To shape the bottom piecrust,* on a lightly floured work surface, roll out the pastry ⅛ inch thick. Using a pastry wheel, cut out a circle 6 inches larger than the diameter of your pie plate. Transfer the pastry to the plate by loosely rolling the pastry around the rolling pin. Starting from one edge of your pie plate, unroll the pastry across the plate, shaping and easing the pastry into the plate as you go. To avoid shrinking, do not stretch the dough. Finish and flute the edge according to your recipe's directions.

(continued on page 126)

FOR ONE 8- TO 9-INCH DEEP-DISH PIECRUST OR 2 REGULAR SINGLE PIECRUSTS

⅓ cup ice water

1 extra-large egg yolk, slightly beaten

1 tablespoon fresh lemon juice

2 cups all-purpose flour

1 cup cake flour

3 tablespoons sugar

1 teaspoon salt

½ teaspoon baking powder

¾ cup (1½ sticks) cold unsalted butter, cut into ½-inch cubes

¼ cup vegetable shortening

FOR EIGHT 4½- OR 5-INCH TARTLET SHELLS

⅓ cup ice water

1 extra-large egg yolk, slightly beaten

1 tablespoon fresh lemon juice

2 cups all-purpose flour

1 cup cake flour

3 tablespoons sugar

1 teaspoon salt

½ teaspoon baking powder

¾ cup (1½ sticks) cold unsalted butter, cut into ½-inch cubes

To shape tartlet shells: Set out eight 4½- to 5-inch tartlet molds with ¾-inch-high sides (preferably nonstick and with removable bottoms). On a lightly floured work surface, roll out the pastry ⅛ inch thick and cut eight 6-inch circles with a pastry wheel. Fit one pastry round into each tartlet mold and press with your fingers around the bottom and sides until the pastry is smooth and there are no visible bubbles. Roll your rolling pin across the top of the mold to trim the shell.

3. *To prebake (blind-bake) a pie shell:* Preheat the oven to 425°F. Prick the crust all over, on the bottom and up the sides, with the tines of a dinner fork to help prevent the crust from shrinking during baking. Loosely line the crust with aluminum foil or parchment paper and half-fill the crust with pie weights (or use dried beans or uncooked rice). Bake for 12 minutes to partially bake and 15 minutes to bake the shell completely. Remove the foil or parchment containing the pie weights, beans, or rice. Check the bottom of the shell. If it still feels soft and wet but the fluted edge is nicely golden, cover the fluted edge with foil, leaving the bottom of the shell uncovered. Return the pie shell to the oven for about 5 more minutes, until it feels dry to the touch. Transfer the crust to a wire rack. Fill the shell and finish the pie as your recipe directs.

To prebake tartlet shells: Preheat the oven to 400°F. Prick the pastry all over with the tines of a fork (this will prevent shrinking). Bake the tartlet shells until golden, about 12 minutes. Transfer the shells to a rack to cool. Fill the shells and finish the tartlets as your recipe directs.

The Junior's Way

Here's a fast tip for building a lattice crust, from the bakers at Junior's. Cut the pastry strips as directed in step 5 on page 83. Place 3 strips on top of the pie, one in the center and one on either side, an equal distance apart. Turn the pie one-third of a circle and lay 3 more strips diagonally on top in the same way. Repeat two more times, using 2 strips instead of 3 each time. Be sure to turn the pie one-third of a circle before laying down the next layer. Now stand back and admire your work!

Junior's loves to decorate the sides and tops of its cakes and cupcakes with cake crumbs. Here is how to do it.

decorator cake crumbs

1. Preheat the oven to 350°F.

2. Set the cake specified in the individual recipe on a baking sheet and break into pieces. Warm it in the oven for 15 to 20 minutes to dry the pieces out, tossing a couple of times with a fork to separate them into crumbs. The time will vary, depending upon how moist the cake is. Watch carefully and do not let them toast. Transfer to a wire rack to cool.

3. *To make medium fine crumbs for decorating cupcakes,* break the pieces with your fingers into crumbs.

For extra-fine crumbs for decorating the side of a layer cake, process the crumbs in a food processor, using the pulse button, until the crumbs are the size you want. They should be fine, but not so small that they are powdery.

The Junior's Way

A 1/2-inch-thick layer of cake trimmed away from the top of an 8- or 9-inch cake layer will give you about 2 cups of fine cake crumbs, enough to cover the side of an 8- or 9-inch 2-layer cake. Trimming away a 1/2-inch layer from 2 cake layers gives about 4 cups of crumbs, enough to cover the side of a 3- or 4-layer cake. This technique also levels the cake layers, giving the cake a very professional look when frosted.

This is one of the simplest—as well as the most versatile and delicious—icings and it keeps popping up on the top of many of Junior's specialties. The most important of its three ingredients is the chocolate. Be sure to buy a top-quality chocolate containing at least 60% cacao. You can also use couverture chocolate if you can find it, which is even more expensive. Junior's uses high-grade, dark bittersweet chocolate.

chocolate ganache

¾ cup heavy cream

6 ounces bittersweet chocolate (at least 60% cacao), coarsely chopped

1 teaspoon pure vanilla extract

MAKES 1 CUP GANACHE (ENOUGH TO FROST AND DECORATE THE TOP AND SIDE OF ONE 8- OR 9-INCH CHEESECAKE OR FROST 8 CUPCAKES)

1. Combine the cream and chocolate in a heavy, medium saucepan and stir over medium-low heat until the chocolate melts and the mixture begins to bubble a little around the side. Quickly whisk the mixture until it comes together into a smooth chocolate sauce. Immediately remove from the heat and whisk in the vanilla.

2. Pour the ganache into a heatproof bowl that can go into the freezer. Freeze just until it thickens, 10 to 15 minutes. Remove from the freezer and use immediately to glaze and ice the cake fast, before the ganache has the chance to thicken too much to spread easily. Ice the side of the cake first, then the top. Work fast to smooth out any irregular bumps in the ganache before it sets.

FOR 1½ CUPS CHOCOLATE GANACHE (ENOUGH TO FILL, FROST, AND DECORATE A 1-LAYER CAKE OR FROST 12 CUPCAKES):

Prepare as directed above, using 1 cup heavy or whipping cream, 8 ounces chocolate, and 1 teaspoon pure vanilla extract.

FOR 2 CUPS CHOCOLATE GANACHE (ENOUGH TO FILL, FROST, AND DECORATE A 2-LAYER CAKE OR FROST 16 CUPCAKES):

Prepare as directed above, using 1½ cups heavy or whipping cream, 12 ounces chocolate, and 1 tablespoon vanilla extract.

FOR 3 CUPS CHOCOLATE GANACHE (ENOUGH TO FILL, FROST, AND DECORATE A 3-LAYER CAKE OR FROST 24 CUPCAKES):

Prepare as directed opposite, using 2 cups heavy or whipping cream, 1 pound chocolate, and 1½ tablespoons vanilla extract.

FOR 4 CUPS CHOCOLATE GANACHE (ENOUGH TO FILL, FROST, AND DECORATE A 4-LAYER CAKE OR FROST 32 CUPCAKES):

Prepare as directed opposite, using 3 cups heavy or whipping cream, 1½ pounds chocolate, and 2 tablespoons vanilla extract.

The Junior's Way

• When icing with ganache, brush away any crumbs from the side and top of the cake before you start and use a revolving cake stand if you have one.

• A narrow metal icing spatula with a long offset handle is the ideal tool. Most are 11 to 12 inches long with a 1-inch-wide metal blade.

• To frost the top of a cake with a thin, smooth layer of ganache, called a "mirror," quickly and evenly pour the ganache from a pitcher over the top of the cake, spreading it out with a spatula if necessary. If you want some drizzles down the side, also pour some ganache near the edge of the cake.

• To give the smoothest finish, warm your spatula under hot running water. Dry it before using to smooth out the ganache.

• For cakes that are not topped with crumbs or other decorations, Junior's often finishes them off by lightly dragging a small spatula in lines across the top, from side to side, about 1 inch apart. This creates shallow decorative ridges all across the top of the cake.

As any cake decorator knows, whipped cream needs to be "just right" when piping it through a pastry bag onto a cake. The perfect decorator's whipped cream is stiff, yet still soft enough to flow through the bag smoothly, evenly, and easily. Both the confectioners' sugar and cream of tartar stabilize the whipped cream to give it a professional look and ensure it will stand up perfectly on the cake. Be sure to refrigerate the cake right after decorating.

decorator's never-fail whipped cream

MAKES 4 CUPS WHIPPED CREAM (ENOUGH TO FILL, FROST, AND DECORATE THE TOP AND SIDE OF AN 8- OR 9-INCH 2-LAYER CAKE)

3 tablespoons confectioners' sugar

½ teaspoon cream of tartar

1 pint (2 cups) icy-cold heavy or whipping cream

2 teaspoons pure vanilla extract

1. Chill the bowl and mixer beaters (this is very important if your kitchen is warm). Mix the sugar and cream of tartar together. Whip the cream in a medium bowl with an electric mixer on high just until it begins to thicken. With the mixer running, add the sugar mixture, then the vanilla, and continue beating until the cream stands up in peaks that are stiff but still soft enough to flow. Don't overbeat at this stage or the cream will curdle. For best results, use immediately or refrigerate and use within 30 minutes.

2. Fit the right size decorating tip onto a pastry bag. Use a coupler to attach them, so you can change the tips easily without cleaning out the bag each time. A few decorating tips are too large for a coupler, so use these larger tips inside a bag with a small hole and fit the tip snugly inside before adding the whipped cream.

For whipped cream rosettes with deep, more decorative ridges, use closed-star tips: #845, #846, or #847 for large rosettes and stars; #30, #35, or #844 for medium-size ones.

For decorations with a "softer" look and fewer details, choose open-star tips: #825, #826, or #827 for large rosettes and stars; #1M, #4B, or #822 for medium-size ones.

3. Put the frosted cake in the freezer for 30 minutes to set the decorations. Transfer to the refrigerator until time to serve.

FOR 6 CUPS DECORATOR'S NEVER-FAIL WHIPPED CREAM (ENOUGH TO FILL, FROST, AND DECORATE A 3-LAYER CAKE):

Prepare as directed opposite, using ⅓ cup confectioners' sugar, ½ teaspoon cream of tartar, 1½ pints (3 cups) icy-cold heavy or whipping cream, and 1 tablespoon pure vanilla extract.

FOR 8 CUPS DECORATOR'S NEVER-FAIL WHIPPED CREAM (ENOUGH TO FILL, FROST, AND DECORATE A 4-LAYER CAKE):

Prepare as directed opposite, using ½ cup confectioners' sugar, ½ teaspoon cream of tartar, 1 quart (4 cups) icy-cold heavy or whipping cream, and 2 tablespoons pure vanilla extract.

The Junior's Way

• From the pastry chef at Junior's comes this tip for filling a pastry bag with whipped cream or frosting. First, fold the top of the bag to form a 1-inch cuff. Fill the bag only about three-fourths full, no more. Unfold the cuff and twist the top tightly. Squeeze the bag over a small bowl for a few seconds, until a burst of air pops out. Now it's ready for piping cream onto the cake. How tightly you squeeze the bag determines not only the amount of cream that flows through the bag into the tip and onto the cake, but also the thickness of the decorations.

• While icing, refrigerate the bowl of extra whipped cream.

This buttercream does it all! Its smooth, creamy consistency gives you plenty of time to swirl it on, and it sets up nicely for easy slicing and serving. You can also use this buttercream for piping rosettes, borders, or thin lines, however fancy you wish. It's soft enough to flow through even the smallest decorating tip but thick enough to make rosettes and borders with plenty of definition.

decorator's buttercream

MAKES 4 CUPS BUTTERCREAM (ENOUGH TO FILL, FROST, AND DECORATE THE TOP AND SIDE OF AN 8- OR 9-INCH 2-LAYER CAKE OR FROST 8 TO 10 CUPCAKES)

4 cups sifted confectioners' sugar (1 pound)

¼ teaspoon salt

1 cup (2 sticks) unsalted butter, at room temperature (important!)

¼ cup vegetable shortening

1 tablespoon light corn syrup

1 tablespoon pure vanilla extract

2 teaspoons fresh lemon juice

3 to 4 tablespoons cold heavy or whipping cream

Assorted food colors, preferably icing gels (optional)

1. Sift the sugar and salt together.

2. Beat the butter and shortening together in a large bowl with an electric mixer on high until creamy, about 3 minutes, scraping the bowl down once or twice. While the mixer is running, beat in the corn syrup, vanilla, and lemon juice. Reduce the speed to low and add the confectioners' sugar in 2 additions. Add 2 tablespoons of the cream and beat on high for 3 minutes. Add more of the cream, 1 tablespoon at a time, as needed to reach spreading consistency. The icing should look light, airy, almost fluffy. To keep the frosting fresh while you work, place a damp paper towel over the top and refrigerate. This is best used within 30 minutes of mixing.

3. Color the icing (optional). Add only a few drops of color at a time. If using gel colors, add a small amount on the tip of a knife, then slice through the bowl to distribute the color throughout. Blend in the color completely before adding more.

4. To decorate: Fit a decorator's pastry bag with a small round tip (#1, #2, or #3) for lines. Use closed-star tips for decorations with more decorative ridges and open-star ones for softer decorations with fewer defined details. Choose a small closed-star tip for small stars (#24 or #26), and a medium closed-star tip (#30, #35, or #844) or a medium open-star tip (#1M, #4B, or #822) for stars, rosettes, shell borders, rosettes, fleurs-de-lis, and wider zigzag lines and for

(continued on page 134)

decorator's buttercream (continued)

icing cupcakes. To finish off the top of a cake with large rosettes, shells, or stars, use a large open-star tip (#825, #826, or #827) or a large closed-star tip (#845, #846, or #847).

FOR 6 CUPS DECORATOR'S BUTTERCREAM (ENOUGH TO FILL, FROST, AND DECORATE A 3-LAYER CAKE OR FROST 12 TO 14 CUPCAKES)

Prepare as directed on page 132, using 6 cups (1½ pounds) sifted confectioners' sugar, ½ teaspoon salt, 1½ cups (3 sticks) unsalted butter (at room temperature), ¼ cup vegetable shortening, 1 tablespoon light corn syrup, 1 tablespoon pure vanilla extract, 1 tablespoon fresh lemon juice, and 5 to 6 tablespoons cold heavy or whipping cream.

FOR 8 CUPS DECORATOR'S BUTTERCREAM (ENOUGH TO FILL, FROST, AND DECORATE A 4-LAYER CAKE OR FROST 16 TO 18 CUPCAKES)

Prepare as directed on page 132, using 8 cups (2 pounds) sifted confectioners' sugar, ½ teaspoon salt, 1 pound (4 sticks) unsalted butter (at room temperature), ½ cup vegetable shortening, 2 tablespoons light corn syrup, 2 tablespoons pure vanilla extract, 1½ tablespoons fresh lemon juice, and 6 to 8 tablespoons cold heavy or whipping cream.

FOR 10 CUPS DECORATOR'S BUTTERCREAM (ENOUGH TO FILL, FROST, AND GENEROUSLY DECORATE A 4-LAYER CAKE OR FROST 20 TO 22 CUPCAKES)

Prepare as directed on page 132, using 10 cups (2½ pounds) sifted confectioners' sugar, 1 teaspoon salt, 1¼ pounds (5 sticks) unsalted butter (at room temperature), ½ cup vegetable shortening, 2 tablespoons light corn syrup, 2 tablespoons pure vanilla extract, 2 tablespoons fresh lemon juice, and 8 to 10 tablespoons cold heavy or whipping cream.

FOR 12 CUPS DECORATOR'S BUTTERCREAM (ENOUGH TO FILL, FROST, AND GENEROUSLY DECORATE A 4-LAYER CAKE WITH A FANCY BORDER OR FROST 24 TO 26 CUPCAKES)

Prepare as directed on page 132, using 12 cups (3 pounds) sifted confectioners' sugar, 1 teaspoon salt, 1½ pounds (6 sticks) unsalted butter (at room temperature), ¾ cup vegetable shortening, 3 tablespoons light corn syrup, 2 tablespoons pure vanilla extract, 2 tablespoons fresh lemon juice, and 10 to 12 tablespoons cold heavy or whipping cream.

The Junior's Way

• The corn syrup in this recipe makes the icing easier to spread.

• Don't skimp on the mixing. Time it according to the recipe.

• If you're going to color the icing, those little pots of concentrated coloring gels are preferable to liquid colors. A very little bit of gel gives a lot of color without watering down the frosting. Look for them at specialty cookery stores or online.

This deep, dark, creamy chocolate buttercream really tastes like chocolate! It's all thanks to the use of good-quality bittersweet chocolate and a helping of cocoa.

junior's fudge frosting

MAKES 4 CUPS FROSTING (ENOUGH TO FILL, FROST, AND DECORATE THE TOP AND SIDE OF AN 8- OR 9-INCH 2-LAYER CAKE OR FROST 8 TO 10 CUPCAKES)

4 cups sifted confectioners' sugar (1 pound)

¼ teaspoon salt

1 cup (2 sticks) unsalted butter, at room temperature (important!)

¼ cup vegetable shortening

2 tablespoons dark corn syrup

1 tablespoon unsweetened dark cocoa powder (100% cacao)

1 tablespoon pure vanilla extract

10 ounces bittersweet chocolate (at least 60% cacao), melted and cooled

3 to 4 tablespoons cold heavy or whipping cream

1. Sift the sugar and salt together.

2. Beat the butter and shortening together in a large bowl with an electric mixer on high until creamy, about 3 minutes, scraping the bowl down once or twice. While the mixer is still running, beat in the corn syrup, cocoa, and vanilla. Blend in the melted chocolate. Reduce the speed to low and add the confectioners' sugar in two additions. Add 2 tablespoons of the cream and beat on high for 3 minutes, adding more of the cream, 1 tablespoon at a time, as needed to reach spreading consistency. The icing should be airy, almost fluffy, with a rich chocolate color. To keep the frosting fresh while you work, place a damp paper towel over the top and refrigerate. This is best used within 30 minutes of mixing.

3. To decorate: Fit a decorator's pastry bag with a small round tip (#1, #2, or #3) for lines. Use closed-star tips for decorations with more decorative ridges and open-star ones for softer decorations with fewer defined details. Choose a small closed-star tip for small stars (such as #22, #24, or #26), and a medium closed-star tip (such as #30, #35, or #844) or a medium open-star tip (such as #1M, 4B, or #822) for stars, rosettes, shell borders, fleurs-de-lis, and wider zigzag lines and for icing cupcakes. To finish off the top of a cake with large rosettes, shells, or stars, use a large open-star tip (such as #825, #826, or #827) or a large closed-star tip (#845, #846, or #847).

FOR 6 CUPS JUNIOR'S FUDGE FROSTING (ENOUGH TO FILL, FROST, AND DECORATE A 3-LAYER CAKE OR FROST 12 TO 14 CUPCAKES):

Prepare as directed above, using 6 cups (1½ pounds) sifted confectioners' sugar, ½ teaspoon salt, 1½ cups (3 sticks) unsalted butter (at room temperature),

(continued on page 136)

junior's fudge frosting (continued)

6 tablespoons vegetable shortening, 1 pound bittersweet chocolate (melted and cooled), 2 tablespoons dark corn syrup, 1½ tablespoons unsweetened dark cocoa powder (100% cacao), 1 tablespoon pure vanilla extract, and 4 to 5 tablespoons cold heavy or whipping cream.

FOR 8 CUPS JUNIOR'S FUDGE FROSTING (ENOUGH TO FILL, FROST, AND DECORATE A 4-LAYER CAKE OR FROST 16 TO 18 CUPCAKES):

Prepare as directed on page 175, using 8 cups (2 pounds) sifted confectioners' sugar, ½ teaspoon salt, 1 pound (4 sticks) unsalted butter (at room temperature), ½ cup vegetable shortening, 1¼ pounds bittersweet chocolate (melted and cooled), 2 tablespoons dark corn syrup, 1½ tablespoons unsweetened dark cocoa powder (100% cacao), 2 tablespoons pure vanilla extract, and 6 to 7 tablespoons cold heavy or whipping cream.

The Junior's Way

• Use a long, narrow metal spatula (about 12 inches long including the handle and 1 inch wide) to frost and decorate large cakes. Use a shorter one (about 8 inches long and ¾ inch wide) for frosting cupcakes and cookies. Offset-handled spatulas are best for these frosting jobs.

• Before you begin icing a cake, brush away any crumbs from the sides and tops of the layers. This gives a smooth, professional look, without any unsightly bubbles or bumps.

Junior's loves cream cheese! So it's no surprise to find them frosting cheese-cakes, butter cakes, even cupcakes with this delicious cream cheese frosting. Like Decorator's Buttercream, it's easy to work with, whether swirling it onto cakes or piping out very fine lines or fancier stars, rosettes, shells, and borders.

junior's cream cheese frosting

MAKES 7 CUPS FROSTING (ENOUGH TO FILL, FROST, AND DECORATE THE TOP AND SIDE OF AN 8- OR 9-INCH 2-LAYER CAKE OR FROST 14 TO 16 CUPCAKES)

4 cups (1 pound) sifted confectioners' sugar

¼ teaspoon salt

1 cup (2 sticks) unsalted butter, at room temperature (important!)

¼ cup vegetable shortening

1 tablespoon light corn syrup

1 tablespoon pure vanilla extract

Two 8-ounce packages Philadelphia cream cheese (use only full fat), at room temperature (important!)

Heavy or whipping cream, if needed

Assorted food colors, preferably icing gels (optional)

1. Sift the sugar and salt together.

2. Beat the butter and shortening together in a large bowl with an electric mixer on high until creamy, about 3 minutes, scraping down the bowl once or twice. While the mixer is running, beat in the corn syrup and vanilla. Reduce the speed to low and add the confectioners' sugar in 2 additions. With the mixer on high, blend in the cream cheese, one package at a time, then beat for 3 minutes more. If needed, add cream, 1 tablespoon at a time, to bring the icing to spreading consistency. The icing should look light, airy, and almost fluffy. To keep the frosting fresh while you work, place a damp paper towel over the top and refrigerate. The frosting is best used within an hour of mixing.

3. Color the icing (optional). Add only a few drops of color at a time. If using gel colors, add a small amount on the tip of a knife, then slice through the bowl to distribute the color evenly throughout. Blend in the color completely before adding more.

4. To decorate: Fit a decorator's pastry bag with a small round tip (#1, #2, or #3) for lines. Use closed-star tips for decorations with more decorative ridges and open-star ones for softer decorations with fewer defined details. Choose a small closed-star tip for small stars (#22, #24, or #26), and a medium closed-star tip (#30, #35, or #844) or a medium open-star tip (#1M, #4B, or #822) for stars, rosettes, shell borders, rosettes, fleurs-de-lis, and wider zigzag lines and

(continued on page 138)

for icing cupcakes. To finish off the top of a cake with large rosettes, shells, or stars, use a large open-star tip (#825, #826, or #827) or a large closed-star tip (#845, #846, #847).

FOR 9 CUPS JUNIOR'S CREAM CHEESE FROSTING (ENOUGH TO FILL, FROST, AND DECORATE A 3-LAYER CAKE OR 18 TO 20 CUPCAKES):

Prepare as directed on page 137, using 6 cups (1½ pounds) sifted confectioners' sugar, ¼ teaspoon salt, 1½ cups (3 sticks) unsalted butter (at room temperature), ½ cup vegetable shortening, 2 tablespoons light corn syrup, 1 tablespoon pure vanilla extract, three 8-ounce packages cream cheese (use only full fat, at room temperature), and heavy or whipping cream as needed.

FOR 11 CUPS JUNIOR'S CREAM CHEESE FROSTING (ENOUGH TO FILL, FROST, AND DECORATE A 4-LAYER CAKE OR FROST 22 TO 24 CUPCAKES):

Prepare as directed on page 137, using 8 cups (2 pounds) sifted confectioners' sugar, ½ teaspoon salt, 1 pound (4 sticks) unsalted butter (at room temperature), ½ cup vegetable shortening, 2 tablespoons light corn syrup, 2 tablespoons pure vanilla extract, four 8-ounce packages cream cheese (use only full fat, at room temperature), and heavy or whipping cream as needed.

The Junior's Way

- While icing and decorating, keep the bowl of extra frosting in the refrigerator.

- If the icing becomes too soft for piping, stir in a little more confectioners' sugar, 1 tablespoon at a time.

- An icing tip: In the decorating section of Junior's bakery, each decorator uses a revolving cake stand that sits on a short pedestal. As the cake turns on the stand, the decorator is able to reach all parts of the cake quickly and easily. To smooth out the icing, the decorator holds her spatula flat against the side of the cake; as she spins the cake around, she smooths out the icing, making each cake look just like the last one—very professional! It's important to apply just the right amount of pressure to the spatula: the more pressure you apply, the more icing you remove.

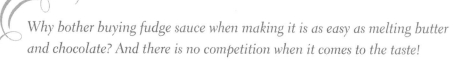

Why bother buying fudge sauce when making it is as easy as melting butter and chocolate? And there is no competition when it comes to the taste!

the best! fudge sauce

MAKES ABOUT 2 CUPS

¼ cup (½ stick) unsalted butter

½ cup firmly packed light brown sugar

1 tablespoon unsweetened dark cocoa powder (100% cacao)

Dash of salt

8 ounces bittersweet chocolate (at least 60% cacao), chopped or broken into small pieces

1 cup heavy or whipping cream

1 tablespoon pure vanilla extract

1. Melt the butter with the brown sugar, cocoa, and salt in a heavy, medium saucepan over medium heat, whisking to combine. Add the chocolate and stir until melted and smooth.

2. Slowly stir in the cream and heat, stirring frequently, until the sauce is smooth and thickens. Watch closely and do not let boil. Remove from the heat and stir in the vanilla. Refrigerate any leftover sauce in an airtight container; it will keep for up to 1 week. To reheat, stir constantly over medium heat until hot.

Junior's uses almond-macaroon crumbs to finish off their fresh berry cheesecakes and pies. They add a little crunch and sweetness to whichever pastry they're sprinkled on. This one has three nuts, instead of just almonds, and sweetened angel-flake coconut, not the shredded kind.

junior's macaroon crunch

MAKES ABOUT 1 CUP

⅔ cup chopped mixed nuts (blanched almonds, pecans, and walnuts)

½ cup sweetened angel-flake coconut

Preheat the oven to 350°F. Toss the nuts and coconut on a rimmed baking sheet until mixed. Toast, tossing 3 or 4 times, until golden and crunchy, 10 to 15 minutes. Transfer to a wire rack to cool.

This sauce is very popular with Junior's regulars. It comes alongside their fresh strawberry shortcake and blintzes. It's used to make Junior's fresh strawberry skyscraper ice cream sodas, and it's layered into the strawberry skyscraper sundaes.

junior's fresh strawberry sauce

MAKES 1 QUART

2 quarts ripe strawberries
1 cup cold water
2 cups sugar
¼ cup cornstarch
1 teaspoon pure vanilla extract
¼ teaspoon pure lemon extract
2 to 3 drops red food coloring (optional)

1. Wash the berries, hull, and pick them over, discarding any over-ripe or under-ripe ones. Slice the berries, vertically, ½ inch thick (see The Junior's Way, below). Place in a medium heatproof bowl; set aside.

2. Bring ¾ cup of the water and all of the sugar to a boil in a heavy medium saucepan over high heat; continue to boil, uncovered, for 5 minutes.

3. Dissolve the cornstarch in the remaining ¼ cup water in a cup. Whisk the cornstarch mixture into the boiling syrup and cook just until it thickens and turns clear, about 2 minutes. Watch closely! If a cornstarch-thickened sauce is cooked too long, the cornstarch will lose its thickening power, as heat can "break" the gel.

4. Remove the syrup from the heat and stir in both extracts. Whisk in the food coloring if you wish. Drizzle the syrup over the berries and gently stir until they are coated. Let cool to room temperature. At that point, you may use the sauce or transfer to an airtight container and refrigerate for up to 3 days. Junior's makes and serves this sauce fresh daily—but if you have some left over, you may freeze it for up to 2 weeks. When defrosted, expect it to be slightly thinner, but it's still fine. Serve cold or at room temperature.

The Junior's Way

Pay close attention when slicing the berries. Slice them vertically from top end to pointed end—½ inch thick, no thinner. This size keeps them plump and juicy in the sauce.

If Your Dessert Is Not Perfect

PROBLEM	PROBABLE CAUSES	SOLUTION
1. *Cheesecake:* The top of my cake cracked during baking.	• The water in the water bath was too hot or boiled dry. This will leave the heat in the oven dry, instead of moist, as is needed for cheesecakes. • Your cheesecake is overbaked. Your oven is probably too hot.	• While your cheesecake is baking, watch the water bath. If the water boils, add a little warm water. Do not let it boil dry! • Use an oven thermometer. Call your range repairman to recalibrate your oven.
2. *Cheesecake:* The top of my cake was perfect when I took it out of the oven, but it cracked as it cooled.	• The ingredients were not mixed in completely. The batter should be smooth—without any visible lumps of cream cheese. • Your cheesecake is overbaked. It baked too long and/or too fast, causing the cake to shrink as it cooled, leaving a deep crack in the center. • You moved the cake too much before it had completely cooled.	• Before putting the batter into the pan, gently stir it with a rubber spatula, lifting it up from the bottom of the bowl and making sure all the ingredients are wet and blended in. • Check your cheesecake after it has baked for 1 hour. The cake is ready to take out of the oven when the edge is set and light golden brown, the top is a light golden tan, and the center is dry, not wet (the center will still be jiggly, but that's OK). • Transfer the cake from the oven to a rack and forget about it! Do not move it for at least 2 to 4 hours.
3. *Cheesecake:* My cake fell in the center while it was cooling.	• Your cake was underbaked. • You refrigerated the cake too soon.	• Cheesecake is done when the edge is light golden brown and the top is an even, light golden tan. The top should be dry, not wet or sticky. • Cool the cake for at least 2 hours and cool to the touch before refrigerating it.
4. *Butter cake/sponge cake:* My cake fell in the center as it cooled.	• The oven temperature was too low. • You took the cake out of the oven before it was done.	• Leave the oven door closed until 5 minutes before the suggested bake time. *No peeking before then!* • Butter and sponge cakes are done when a pick inserted in the center comes out almost clean, with a few moist crumbs attached.
5. *Butter cake:* My cake looks fine on the top but has tunnels and large air holes throughout when I slice it.	• You may have used too much baking powder or baking soda. • The batter was overbeaten.	• Check your recipe and use only the amount of baking powder or baking soda called for. *Measure it carefully!* • Beat the flour and liquid in by hand, with a wooden spoon, unless the recipe specifies an electric mixer.
6. *Cupcakes:* My cupcakes looked great when I took them out of the oven, but they fell in the center as they cooled.	• Your cupcakes were underbaked.	• Bake cupcakes until a pick inserted in the center comes out almost clean, with a few moist crumbs attached.
7. *Pie pastry:* The dough sticks to the rolling pin when I try to roll it out.	• The dough is too warm.	• Return the dough to the refrigerator and chill it until it feels cold, but is still pliable enough to roll.

PROBLEM	PROBABLE CAUSES	SOLUTION
8. *Blind-baked piecrust:* The edge of the crust shrank and lost its nice fluting during baking.	• You may have stretched the dough when you fitted it into the pie plate.	• Fit the pastry loosely in the pie plate—no stretching!
9. *Blind-baked piecrust:* The crust puffed up as it baked.	• The crust was not pricked enough before baking. • The crust was not weighed down during baking.	• Be sure to prick the side as well as the bottom of the piecrust. Freeze the crust for 15 minutes before baking. • Use pie weights.
10. *Custard pie:* The custard curdled when I cooked it.	• The custard is overcooked. You may not have tempered the egg yolks enough before adding them to the hot custard. • You used too high a heat to cook the custard.	• Follow the recipe and add enough hot liquid to the egg yolks to warm them before stirring them into the custard in the saucepan. • Cook custard over medium heat (no hotter!) and stir constantly, just until it thickens. Remove from the heat immediately.
11. *Custard pie:* My pie cracked in the center while it was cooling.	• Your pie was overbaked. • Your oven was probably too hot.	• Take the pie out of the oven when a knife inserted in the center comes out almost clean but still moist, not dry. • Use an oven thermometer. Your oven may need recalibration.
12. *Fruit pie:* My pie looked cooked, but the filling was runny when I cut it.	• You probably did not cool the pie long enough.	• Fruit pies, such as apple, cherry, or peach, need at least 4 to 6 hours to cool at room temperature before slicing.
13. *Cut-out sugar cookies:* My cookies stick to the work surface and are hard to transfer to the baking sheets without tearing them.	• Your dough is probably too warm. • You rolled the dough too thin. • You did not use floured cookie cutters. • You did not use a spatula to transfer the cookies to the baking sheet.	• When rolling, take out only one piece of dough at a time and leave the rest to chill in the refrigerator. • Roll the dough out ⅜ inch thick. • Dip your cookie cutters into flour frequently when cutting out the cookies. • Transfer cookies to the baking sheet with a metal spatula (don't try to pick them up with your hands).
14. *Egg cream:* The foam on my egg cream isn't very high.	• The seltzer is not cold, fresh, and bubbly. • You started stirring the egg cream too soon and/or may not have stirred vigorously enough.	• Use only icy-cold milk and seltzer when making egg creams. Use only seltzer from a new, unopened bottle. • Fill the glass three-fourths full with seltzer, without stirring, then start stirring vigorously—both clockwise and up and down—until a thick, white head of foam rises to the top.
15. *Chocolate egg cream:* The foamy head is a muddy brown color instead of white.	• If you stir a chocolate egg cream too soon, the chocolate syrup mixes with the milk first, so you're stirring seltzer into chocolate (not white) milk. This turns the foam brown.	• Wait until you have filled the glass three-fourths full with seltzer before stirring the egg cream, so you are adding seltzer to white (not chocolate) milk. The foam will be white.

Metric Equivalents

LIQUID/DRY MEASURES	
U.S.	**METRIC**
¼ teaspoon	1.25 milliliters
½ teaspoon	2.5 milliliters
1 teaspoon	5 milliliters
1 tablespoon (3 teaspoons)	15 milliliters
1 fluid ounce (2 tablespoons)	30 milliliters
¼ cup (4 tablespoons)	60 milliliters
⅓ cup (5⅓ tablespoons)	80 milliliters
½ cup (8 tablespoons)	120 milliliters
1 cup (16 tablespoons)	240 milliliters
1 pint (2 cups)	480 milliliters
1 quart (4 cups; 32 ounces)	960 milliliters
1 gallon (4 quarts)	3.84 liters
1 ounce (by weight)	28 grams
1 pound	454 grams
2.2 pounds	1 kilogram

OVEN TEMPERATURES		
°F	**GAS MARK**	**°C**
250	½	120
275	1	140
300	2	150
325	3	165
350	4	180
375	5	190
400	6	200
425	7	220
450	8	230
475	9	240
500	10	260
550	Broil	290

Index

The following companies provided the props for the photographs.

Beth Allen: antique cookie cutters; Arzberg Porcelain furnished by EU Design Distributors (www.eudesignllc.com): Cucina Basic mug, Cucina Basic plate, Cucina Points tumbler, Form 2006 espresso cups and snack saucers, Form 1382 tray, Gourmet bowl, My First Arzberg Colour plate, Profi creamer, Profi cup and saucer, Standard Cult teapot and plates, Standard Profi plate and cafe au lait cup, Standard tray, Tric plates, Tric platter and coffee pot; Fishs Eddy (www.fishseddy.com): bowl, creamer, Mosser Glass Crystal cake stand, Mosser Glass Jadite cake stand, Mosser Glass Vaseline cake stand; Junior's Restaurants: cake stands, coffee cups and saucers, egg cream glasses, napkins; LSA International (www.lsa-international.com): Edel champagne flutes, Klara cake stand, Vienna cake stand and dome; Red Vanilla (www.redvanilla.com): Naturally Vanilla plate; The Sugar Diva (www.thesugardiva.com): cupcake papers, gingham bag, straws; TAG (www.tagltd.com): Pedestal cake stand